Praise HIM WHILE YOU WAIT

PRAISE HIM WHILE YOU WAIT
4th Edition

Publishing Information:

Scripture Music Group Publishing
123 West Bloomingdale Avenue
Brandon, Florida 33511
4th Edition, Edit by Cynthia Ahmed
Book Cover & Graphics by Joseph Anthony

Atiya's Light Publishing
412 North Main Street, Suite 100
Buffalo, Wyoming 82834
www.atiyaslight.com
info@atiyaslight.com
2nd Edition, Edit by Dominique Lambright

Your support and respect for the property of this author is much appreciated.
NOTE: *All scriptures cited in this book are from the King James Version of the Bible unless otherwise noted.*

Library of Congress Control Number: 2019916967
ISBN: 978-1-7365465-0-5

I would like to dedicate this book to the entire World Assemblies Fellowship International (W.A.F.I.) family. A special thank you to all of my children for believing in me and supporting me in everything I've done. It is my sincere prayer that all will be given grace and deliverance, that all will fulfill their purpose in the body of Christ.

Acknowledgments

I am so thankful that God allows me to offer Him praise, it is an honor to minister His Word. Thank you to all of the members of World Assemblies Fellowship International (W.A.F.I.) for your continued support. It is a blessing to serve in ministry; and I am appreciative of your encouragement and faithfulness to the mission.

To my husband, Bishop M.B. Jefferson, thank you for always being there to support me in everything that God has called me to do. I am grateful for your steadfast love and leadership.

I would also like to thank my son, Pastor Calvin Jefferson, for showing forth true servanthood. Bishop and I appreciate your help and demonstration of what a true servant is every day.

Table of Contents

Introduction

My desire for every reader is that after meditating on the contents of this book, that you will be encouraged to manifest your dreams. It is important that I begin by reflecting on two vital scriptures, which will lay the foundation for what I'm about to share. In reading Philippians 4:13 and Luke 17:6, I pray that you will understand how to achieve a successful outcome in whatever you endeavor to accomplish in life. All too often, when people have a yearning to realize a personal goal or dream, they allow doubt, negative self-talk, and limited thinking to interfere. This doubt can wreak havoc on their self-confidence and faith. Yet, self-confidence and faith are two fundamental principles that undergird victory and success on all levels. Possessing confidence in the abilities God has given you, produces determination and endurance. You must have faith that success and victory are possible. Even when the going gets tough, there should be a deep conviction which lies within your heart, that no carnal mind can comprehend. This steadfast trust in God will inspire you to keep going.

Philippians 4:13 states, "I can do all things through Christ who strengthens me." In this text, it lays out the premise that it is not our own strength, but the strength of one much greater than you or me, which gives us the wherewithal to achieve victory over failure.

Further, Luke 17:6 states, "And the Lord said, If ye had faith as a grain of mustard seed, ye might say unto this sycamine tree, Be thou plucked up by the root, and be thou planted in the sea; and it should obey you." This passage in Luke encourages us to have just a little bit of faith in what we set out to do and we can accomplish it, no matter how great or small the task.

There is power in faith; and while it takes courage to dream big, it takes immeasurable perseverance to keep going after our dreams, even in the face of defeat. Faith helps us to remain steadfast and firm on the path to our destiny; and while we may face doubt and even defeat, to square off and look it straight in the eyes and say to that mountain, "Be removed!" Afterwards, looking back only to say, "Glory be to God, look at not what I have done, but look at what God has done."

On the journey through this book, I intend to show you how to calm the winds of doubt and shatter any limited thinking that might have you paralyzed in your tracks, hindering you from going after your dreams. All you have to do is approach it with an open mind and heart. Allow the Spirit of God to move through you and all things become possible.

Perhaps you feel your dreams are too lofty? They seem too heavy or big for you. Nothing is too big for God! There are no limits to what He can do. Our thoughts and ways are not God's thoughts and ways. Remember that. He cannot be contained in the ordinary restrictions of our minds. He sits in the North, yet He flows from the East. He is so vast. His greatness extends from glory to glory, everlasting to everlasting, without end. You trying to limit Him in your life is like trying to restrict the measure of His capabilities. His depth and height cannot be measured. He stretches far beyond our capacity and soars where no man has ever been. There is no end to His omnipotence. It's important to realize that God is GOD and our natural minds are unable to conceive His power. He causes the greatest of scientists to be mystified in their calculations and perplexed enough to realize, there is none like Him. He can cause a baby to grow on the inside of a mother's womb and at the same time make time itself stand still. He is God! The great… 'I AM'.

As you read on, I want you to consider the innocent characteristics of children. We, as adults, can take a page out of their books. Take account of how they play and imagine their future when they get older. Children dream big! They don't place limits on what they can do. They believe they can accomplish anything. Even though sometimes their imaginations may run wild, life experiences don't get in the way or convince them that what they want to achieve is impossible. Children's faith is pure and void of doubt. They are internally nurtured to believe that anything is possible. The world they know is one of love and trust.

When they fall down, they get back up. Parents may kiss away the pain and wipe away their tears, but after that, they get right back out there and try again! Unless something traumatic happens, children don't doubt what they want to do or be when they grow up. They have no question of whether or not their dreams will at some point in their lives become a reality. If you watch them when they play, you can see this. It is the wonderment of childhood; in the innocence of child-like fantasies that the gift of being able to dream, hope, and wish are birthed. In a child's mind, there is no such thing as "this is too big, too great or too small."

Yet, as many children grow and mature somewhere along the way; their parents, teachers, family members, friends, or someone else comes along and shatters their hopes and dreams. Often, these words spoken vicariously plant a seed of doubt in their minds. Their little world and minds are hijacked, by marginalized adults who project their own insecurities and shortcomings onto them by saying statements like; "It was only a dream" or "Fairytales don't come true." Inadvertently, transferring their fear or disappointments onto their young minds because their own dreams of the past may have been shattered. Along the way, these adult persons somehow lost faith in what is possible; becoming discouraged to dream and hope again.

Yet, some people can overcome the negative chatter and discouragement around them. There are some that, regardless of what is said to them or what was done to them, continue to remain steadfast and turn their dreams into reality. Despite the obstacles they've had to face, they continue to believe in God. By doing so, great things are birthed because they dared to believe in their dreams.

When the visions of your life or your dreams are combined with faith, you can move mountains. Some people accomplish much, simply because they do not lose sight of the vision nor the faith in their heart. They moved those mountains of doubt and their life ultimately became evidence of their belief. The Bible says, "Now faith is the substance of things hoped for; the evidence of things not seen," (Heb. 11:1).

According to Webster, a *dream* is a succession of images, thoughts, or emotions passing through the mind during sleep. God gives us dreams to accomplish His purpose. The dreams that God places in each of us are consistent with His Word. Your destiny and your dreams are intricately tied together. You have the power within you to accomplish your purpose. The power within you is the supernatural strength of God, working in you to do what you have been born to do. It is written, "Now unto Him that is able to do exceeding abundantly above all that we ask or think, according to the power that worketh in us," (Eph. 3:20).

God created us from the dust of the Earth and as a result our DNA is filled with power, we are His offspring. Our dreams, thoughts, and emotions are the conduits for new ideas to flow. When you have faith and belief in God, you can put a plan into motion to accomplish your goal. God will create ways for that dream to come true. Usually, the vision will line up with your God-given gifts and talents because this is His way of equipping and preparing you for the purpose placed within you. He will never leave you without provision for the vision. "Every good gift and every perfect gift is from above and cometh down from the Father of lights, with whom is no variableness, neither shadow of turning," (Jas. 1:17).

The Scripture says in Proverbs 18:16 that your gift will make room for you. So, how dare you doubt the power of God in your life? Have you ever tried to fit something too big inside of something too small? Try setting boundaries on something that has no end. Well, that's exactly what happens when you attempt to restrict the power of the Almighty.

Sure, circumstances and obstacles may come to distract or frustrate you, but never allow your dreams to be snatched or stolen. Never allow your hope to be deflated or your vision clouded. Remember that God placed it there in your heart, and the same God will help you to realize it.

Be encouraged and understand that every challenge contains a solution. Walk in the conviction that it is already done, all you are doing is going through the process. As a renowned author has said in his book entitled, *7 Habits of Highly Effective People*, "Begin with the end in mind." Walk like it is already done. Walk in your wealthy place in God. As you stand on His Word, watch everything you could have ever imagined come into fruition. Your wealthy place in God is not only finances and prosperity, but a place of peace in God. Knowing that whatever He has promised shall come to pass. Therefore, remove the limits! In God, there are none!

As you meditate on this book, it is my prayer for you to be filled with a righteous zeal to embrace the dreams God has given you. **Each "course" or chapter that you read will allow you to meditate on specific principles, therefore opening your understanding as we study more in depth together.** Be refreshed in your spirit and mind through His Word. The God in you will work to bring your dreams to pass. Your faith along with works will produce everything you need to fulfill His plan for your life. As you move forward in this process, remember the words of John, "Ye are of God, little children, and have overcome them: because greater is He that is in you, than he that is in the world," (Jn. 4:4).

Course 1

God and His Word is An Anchor

"Which hope we have as an anchor of the soul, both sure and stedfast, and which entereth into that within the [vail]," (Heb. 6:19).

"Let not your heart be troubled: ye believe in God, believe also in me," (Jn. 14:1).

As we begin this journey into each Course, I will present you with a proposition, or rather biblical truths for you to think about. Afterwards, inviting you to apply those guiding principles discussed in any given Course to your life and/or circumstance. Here in Course One, the principle which I would like to highlight is: *God and His Word is An Anchor.* Being secure and stable in your faith as you walk with God, is a principle that guides the concepts shared, in Course One. Let's take a look.

God is our salvation. His Word is the permanence needed to stabilize all areas of our lives. Sometimes when you are going through hardships and struggles, it is difficult to see [as they say], "the forest from the trees." However, asking yourself the right questions, will lead you down the path of finding Truth and ultimately finding Christ.

In 2 Chronicles 7:14 it says, "If my people, which are called by my name, shall humble themselves, and pray, and seek my face, and turn from their wicked ways; then will I hear from Heaven, and will forgive their sin, and will heal their land."

Many people are in need of a healing in their life. Yet, prior to healing, the first question you must ask yourself is, "Why am I struggling?" See, often as believers we want to get to the prize or obtain the victory, but we rarely get excited about the struggle. Yet, the Bible teaches us that the race is neither to the swift nor the strong but to those who can endure until the end (Eccl. 9:11; Matt. 24:13).

There is a reason for every struggle. Knowing the purpose of the conflicts and battles in your life will give you the necessary insight to overcome them. In order to gain the victory, you must conquer setbacks, obstacles and all that comes with it. Imagine a baby who is just learning to walk. They fall down, they get back up, they fall down, and they get back up. This is the repeated pattern that is demonstrated by the baby before actually getting the hang of walking. In the beginning stages of them walking, they stumble a lot and for any parent it can be unnerving because of the unsteadiness of their manner. They are wobbly, shifting back and forth, and from side-to-side as they work to get their balance. This is what a new life in Christ can be like. "A saint is just a sinner who got back up." Everyone makes mistakes in life and everyone has a time in life when they are down. Yet, the blessing can be found in the struggle to get back up. Struggle is the preparation and the process which helps you to walk upright and be strong in the Lord. All things are possible in Christ. You just have to believe and hold on when you are going through your trials.

The Bible instructs us in Mathew 18:3, that unless you come as a little child, you shall not enter the Kingdom of

Heaven. Reading further, in Matthew 19:14 it says, "But Jesus said, suffer little children, and forbid them not, to come unto me: for of such is the Kingdom of Heaven."

In your life, you may be going through all sorts of issues. Yet, through the storms, God is not only helping you to get fit for a greater purpose but He is showing you the possibility in what seems to be impossible. He is turning your mess into a message and your test into a testimony so that others can be saved through your deliverance.

I have heard numerous stories of the unbelievable struggles and suffering that women have gone through. From molestation, to domestic abuse, prostitution, drugs, sick children, living years in physical pain to God only knows. Women often suffer in silence, having to endure trying circumstances and as a result many of those issues come to the surface to be healed.

When I reflect over my own life, it was only God and the love of Christ that helped me to overcome. Through His grace, I was able to make the impossible possible. I got married at seventeen years old, at the urging of my mother and in that relationship I suffered all sorts of abuse. I remember being dragged by my hair, being cursed out, punched in the eye and almost losing it. Prior to that, I was abused by my step-father. I went from one household of abuse and into another.

I was three months into my first marriage when my mother lost her life at the hands of my step-father. I was young and overwhelmed with grief, it tore me apart. I remember saying: "I don't know how to be a mother. I don't know how to be a wife." At the funeral of my mother, my step-father didn't even shed a tear. On top of that, there appeared to be no remorse. I hated him for taking my mother and for what he did to us.

I lost my younger sister when she was in her early 30's to bone cancer. The loss of my mother then my sister was disheartening. I seemed to transition from one trial to another, then the next. Present day, I have a son who is in prison, and although he is now pastoring while serving his time and helping to save souls; I am still believing and trusting God for his physical freedom. So, like the women I minister to, I also know all about suffering. I know all about struggling and working to overcome issues because there have been many storms in my life.

I realize that sometimes when you are going through difficulties, it can seem crushing. Things can get so cloudy to where you can't see a way out. In my distress, I remember crying out to God. I was blinded by pain and anger. However, I can testify today, that while in life we may go through many storms, after the raging downpour - the sun does come out again. So whatever you are going through in your life, drop your anchor and hold onto God's Word. Let the Lord take the wheel. He's going to help you navigate to freedom, sailing you through your storm right onto dry land. If you remain anchored in your faith, He will deliver you and the world will know that He is a Mighty God.

God can do anything but fail. The Bible says in 1 Peter 5:10, "But the God of all grace, who hath called us unto His eternal glory by Christ Jesus, after that ye have suffered a while, make you perfect, stablish, strengthen, settle you."

You might have heard the saying, "When it rains, it pours." Sometimes the struggles and trials seem to be so overwhelming that you start asking God, "Why?" You start crying out to God because it seems too heavy of a load to carry by yourself. Yet, God does not place a burden on you beyond your ability to sustain (1 Cor. 10:13).

Remember, you are never alone. Consider yourself blessed if you are going through issues, simply for who you are in Christ. Ungodly forces often target those who have a purpose in God, trying to hinder positive change and prevent the deliverance of others. Your struggle is not in vain nor is it strange to God. You are in good company, among men and women alike who are trusting Him in the midst of difficult circumstances.

"Beloved, think it not strange concerning the fiery trial which is to try you, as though some strange thing happened unto you: But rejoice, inasmuch as ye are partakers of Christ's sufferings; that, when His glory shall be revealed, ye may be glad also with exceeding joy," (1 Pet. 4:12-13).

When you cry out to the Most High, He performs miracles for you. You see, the suffering that you have gone through or may be going through will lead you to your crown, but you have to hold on. You can't let go or give up. All you have to do is move over and let God steer you in the right direction. Abide in the ship. Don't jump out, just move over! Be joyous in the midst of the storm, remaining steadfast and believing in the promise that God made to you (Acts 27:25).

After all I have been through, from losing my mother to being abused and beat down in my first marriage. I stood up and made a decision to believe God. I "dropped my anchors." I didn't know how He would do it, but I believed in the promises that God had for my life. All I had was the Word. That was all I knew! God answered my prayers before I even finished praying. I stayed the course and remained firm in my beliefs. I praised God in the midst of my trials and waited on Him. I started having Bible study in my living room, even though I was still in struggling with fear and in bondage. In spite of how I felt and how it looked, I believed in and stood on the Word of God. The Word told me that, "...what things soever ye desire, when ye pray, believe that ye receive them, and ye shall have them," (Mrk. 11:24).

After all was said and done, I realized that I had to forgive and that was really hard for me. I lived with the torment of my step-father killing my mother. I hated this man and to have to forgive him. . . God had to deal with me on that. I knew I had to let the hurt go, but it was not easy.

My sister was at a tent revival in Quincy, Florida where she met Bishop M.B. Jefferson, who God had instructed to stop at the assembly. After the service, she invited him to the Bible Study that I was having the next evening. The Bishop came to the Bible Study as invited and during the meeting he began to minister and prophesy to a few people around the room. I distinctly remember that he turned around and looked at me, walking over as if he could feel my pain and what I was going through. He said, "I see you praying and praying and praying and it looks like your prayers are bouncing off of the wall. But after this night, you will never be same."

Prior to the Bishop laying hands on me, I was bound by an overwhelming spirit of fear. I was afraid of many things: driving, people, and even afraid to clap my hands or praise. Before that night, I felt imprisoned and caged. It was like I was locked behind bars and standing there with my hands on the cell bars shouting, "Please can anybody, somebody help me? Can anybody help me? Somebody please let me out!" I was chained up, with chains all on my hands and feet. When Bishop prayed for me, it was as if all of the chains dropped off. When I came to, I felt lighter and my thoughts were clear. This was so real! God told me that He delivered me. I'm telling you; my spirit and mind were unlocked that day. I was instantly set free.

After about six months, I began sharing aspects of my life with the Bishop. I opened up to him about my mother and my step-father and all the things that happened to me. In his wisdom, he told me that I had to let everything go. Anybody that you hate or dislike, you have to let it go. You must forgive others in order for God to hear your prayers.

The Bishop shared with me that God had spoken with him and instructed him to start a ministry in Quincy. After that encounter, God did a quick work. Ultimately, that is when I began ministering at that church. Forty years later, I have transitioned to a different city and assignment, even now giving God all the glory.

That was a difficult season in my life. I was standing in the midst of a storm and suffering because I was holding on to a whole lot of *stuff* . . . unforgiveness, anger, pride. Yet, through God's instructions to Bishop, my life changed for the better. I gained clarity of why I was suffering and instructions on how to be free. Now I say this to you, whatever bondage you are in and whatever storm you are going through, God has you in the palm of His hand. You have to let the Father take the wheel. He's got it! You have to tame the tongue and release everything that needs to be removed in your life. Release those weights and burdens you are carrying. To overcome the storms in your life successfully, you have to stand still. Continue to put God first. Be sure in your beliefs, steadfast in your prayers, and steady in your actions. **Sure… steadfast… and steady!**

The Bible says that you have to come as a little child and in such a state you have access to God. When you examine children, they are coachable and teachable. They are innocent and full of wonder. They play and have fun; they look at the world through hopeful and optimistic eyes.

So what I'm sharing with you is the same thing that the Angel told Paul and Paul told the people: *Abide in the ship!* Hold on and don't let go! The storms will come but if you stay in the ship, you will be saved (Acts 27:20-44).

No matter how bad things appear to be in a given moment, be courageous and of good cheer. God will deliver you, but you have to cry out for His help. "Call unto me, and I will answer thee, and [show] thee great and mighty things, which thou knowest not," (Jer. 33:3).

People are going to say all sorts of things about you and about your situation, but it is important not to get caught up in the negativity, the pessimism, or disputes. Believe God and believe that nothing can happen before His Word hits the ground. In Philippians, the Bible teaches us that God works in people for His will and for His pleasure. He is working in us every single day. It is important to do everything without moaning and quarreling (Phil. 2:13-14). Don't allow yourself to get consumed with doubt; God will deliver you from the situation. Trust Him!

The struggles that happen in life are meant to happen. You just need to be ready! Be prepared in the knowledge of who He is and the tactics of the enemy. Stay the course. The suffering you endure helps to produce perseverance; and perseverance builds character, and character inspires hope (Rom. 5:2-4).

When all 'hell' is breaking loose in your life; *Drop Your Anchor*. An ***anchor*** makes a ship steady and stable by fixing or securing it in place. This also applies to our faith during trying times. You are going to have storms in your life; stay anchored. Remember after reading this book, that when the troubles of life come, stay anchored! Christ holds you in place because He is sure, steadfast, and steady.

There are four types of "anchors" that will get you through the storm and onto the other side. They are belief, prayer, praise, and patience.

1. **Belief** – Believe in God and His Word. The Word helps mature your faith and keeps you focused on what is possible.

2. **Prayer** – Go boldly to the throne of grace and God will have mercy and show you grace in your time of need (Heb. 4:16).

3. **Praise** – Praise God in your circumstances. He will not fail you. Praise confuses the enemy and through your praise God deals with you wondrously. He will never make you look ashamed (Jl. 2:26-27).

4. **Patience** – Exercise patience when going through the trials. Remain hopeful with joy in your heart, being reassured that God's promises are true. Wait on God, He can do anything but fail. Although you may feel in despair and in pain, this is only for a short time. The trials come to purify you and to test your faith. To see how genuine you are in what you say you believe. Your faith is worth more than gold, because even though gold is purified by fire, it can still melt away. Yet, your faith remains. It brings about praise, honor, and glory to God, and becomes a testament of the power of Christ Jesus (Rom. 8:25; 1 Pet. 1:6-7).

When you allow God to take hold of the stern and you drop the anchor, you are saying: "Okay God, you are now in control of my life." You turn everything over to Him. If He says go left, you go left. If He says go right, you go right. If He says go straight ahead, you go straight ahead. You have to love God with all your heart, soul, mind, and strength (Deut. 6:4-7; Matt. 22:37-40; Mrk. 12:30-31). When you turn it over to Him and release control - your problems, your life, and your family become God's business. It's about the Kingdom and ultimately God getting the glory. In Him, nothing is impossible. Even when the winds are contrary, the waters may be rough, let the Father have the wheel. Lighten your load. Release all that may be weighing you down: pride, arrogance, anger, fear, resentment, bitterness. . . Release it all. Let it go! It may look like you are going to sink, but God said lighten the load, control your words and the tongue, do whatever is necessary to make it to the other side of your storm.

He will make the impossible possible, but you have to do it His way. Whether it is in your finances, your marriage, your family, your health, whatever you are believing God for, IT IS done… *if* you believe it can be done. Even so, it will be done in God's time. So, it requires you to be patient.

There is a path for every blessing, but you have to keep the faith even in the midst of the storm. "Now faith is the substance of things hoped for, the evidence of things not seen," (Heb. 11:1). God and His Word is the anchor. So whatever is going on in your life, remember that God's promises remain true and hold fast to His unchanging hand!

WORDS OF EMPOWERMENT

1. Move over and allow God in the driver seat of your life. He has plans for your life and He will make the impossible possible. "For I know the plans I have for you, declares the Lord, plans to prosper you and not harm you, plans to give you hope and a future," (*New International Version,* Jer. 29:11).

2. Continue to dream and live by faith. Do not be ashamed of the hope God has set before you. "For I am not ashamed of the Gospel of Christ: for it is the power of God unto salvation to everyone that believeth; to the Jew first, and also to the Greek. For therein is the righteousness of God revealed from faith to faith: as it is written, the just shall live by faith," (Rom. 1:16-17).

3. The more we proclaim what the Word of God has promised, the more we move from hopelessness to faith. "But what saith it? The Word is nigh thee, even in thy mouth, and in thy heart: that is, the Word of faith, which we preach; That if thou shalt confess with thy mouth the Lord Jesus, and shalt believe in thine heart that God hath raised Him from the dead, thou shalt be saved. For with the heart man believeth unto righteousness; and with the mouth confession is made unto salvation," (Rom. 10:8-10).

4. Whatever you speak will bring life or death, good or bad. Be careful with your words and speaking contrary to His Word. Eliminate the carnal way of thinking, and give life to a new you. A new way of thinking and living. "Death and life are in the power of the tongue: and they that love it shall eat the fruit thereof," (Prov. 18:21).

5. A word not spoken is a word not born. Speak good things! The outward man may get weary, but that inward man becomes stronger and stronger day by day (2 Cor. 4:16-18).

6. Refrain from being discouraged by what you physically see, instead walk by faith (2 Cor. 5:7). God will make the darkness, light. "For thou wilt light my candle: the LORD my God will enlighten my darkness," (Ps. 18:28). The Word of God is a lamp unto our feet and a light unto our path (Ps. 119:105).

7. In order for your dream to manifest, it must have light. "But all things that are reproved are made manifest by the light: for whatsoever doth make manifest is light. Wherefore, He saith, Awake thou that sleepest, and arise from the dead, and Christ shall give thee light," (Eph. 5:13-14). Give thanks for your dream and for salvation. It shall be, even as it were told to you. "Speaking to yourselves in psalms and hymns and spiritual songs, singing and making melody in your heart to the Lord; giving thanks always for all things unto God and the Father in the name of our Lord Jesus Christ," (Eph. 5:19-20).

8. Allow God to be in control of your life. "For none of us liveth to himself, and no man dieth to himself. For whether we live, we live unto the Lord; and whether we die, we die unto the Lord: whether we live therefore, or

die, we are the Lord's. For to this end Christ both died, and rose, and revived, that He might be Lord both of the dead and living," (Rom.14:7-9). We must have a strong confidence in His Word until the end or until we receive our promise. When troubles come, go through. You will reap if you faint not (Gal. 6:9). Rest in the Lord and He shall give you the desires of your heart. In His rest, there is peace. Believe until the end, that the work was laid before the foundation of the world. We must be confident and steadfast unto the end (Heb. 3:6-14).

9. "John answered and said, A man can receive nothing, except it be given him from Heaven," (Jn. 3:27). Christ is able to supply all our needs according to His riches in glory by Christ Jesus. "Do not err, my beloved brethren. Every good gift and every perfect gift is from above, and cometh down from the Father of lights, with whom is no variableness, neither shadow of turning," (Jas. 1:16-17).

10. Wait on the Lord. What you desire of good shall come to pass. Nurture the seed of your ideas with faith and the Word of God. Speak of your dreams, as if they were before your eyes. The Scripture says to call those things

which be not as though they were. You are taken and snared by the words of your mouth. Remove the weeds of negativity. Sing forth a grateful praise for all God has and is doing in your life.

11. You can do all things through Christ Jesus who strengthens you. Magnify the name of God and give Him standing in your life. Give Him an opportunity to perform miracles. He can do anything but fail; but you have to cry out to Him (Phil. 4:10-20).

COURSE ONE DAILY AFFIRMATIONS

- I will not give up and settle for something less than what God wants for me.
- I will speak to every mountain that attempts to hinder my dreams and command them in Jesus' name to be cast away from me.
- I am the victor and not a victim.
- I will praise and not complain.
- I will declare it is not my ability, but it is the God within me.
- I will declare Ephesians 3:20.

- I wait in expectancy for my dreams to be fulfilled.
- I know God is faithful to His promises.
- I will not listen to negative words which seek to discourage me.
- I will put legs to my faith because faith without works is dead.
- I will remain hopeful at all times.
- I will not allow setbacks or disappoints to keep me from pressing forward and believing God.
- I will keep a journal of my dreams, promises, and prophetic words God has spoken to me.
- I will keep the word 'Never' from my vocabulary.
- I will write out my dreams and record their progress (Hab. 2:2-3).

Study Scriptures to Strengthen You

1 Corinthians 13:13

Jeremiah 29:11

James 5:11

Jeremiah 5:16-18

Acts 14:17

Acts 27:20-44

1 Peter 1:6

1 Peter 4:12

1 Peter 5:10

Daniel 9:21

Joshua 23:10

Romans 4:16-21

Romans 8:25

Psalm 52:9

Psalm 57:2

Mark 9:23

Mark 11:24

Hebrews 6:18

Proverbs 15:13-15

Romans 1:16-17

Romans 5:1-2

2 Corinthians 4:6-13, 17

Course 2

I Will Praise Him While I Wait

"And be not drunk with wine, wherein is excess; but be filled with the Spirit; Speaking to yourselves in psalms and hymns and spiritual songs, singing and making melody in your heart to the Lord; Giving thanks always for all things unto God and the Father in the name of our Lord Jesus Christ," (Eph. 5:18-20).

"All thy works shall praise thee, O Lord; and thy saints shall bless thee. They shall speak of the glory of thy Kingdom, and talk of thy power; To make known to the sons of men His mighty acts, and the glorious majesty of His Kingdom," (Ps. 145:10-12).

In Course One, we declared that God and His Word is an anchor. We discussed God's Word being the stability needed to stabilize all areas of life. In this Second Course, we will touch on singing praise with a thankful heart. It is important to always pray and praise God. Continually singing forth with a grateful praise for all that God has done, is doing, and will do in your life. We will have a look into "why" praise is essential and how it can be used to defend against spiritual attacks. We will take the time to delve into the necessity of praise and the power behind it.

As we take this next step together, the proposition I would like for you to consider is the action of praise. Therefore, the guiding principle of Course Two is the affirmation: *I will praise Him while I wait.*

To affirm something is to make steady; strengthen; confirm or firm it up. When we praise God, we reinforce our relationship with Him, while also breaking entrapments and snares that the enemy tries to establish.

So let's talk about praise. The root word of praise means value, worth, or prize. When you "praise" God, you are demonstrating that you value Him, acknowledging the undeniable worth of His presence in your life. You are emphasizing the power and authority of an entity of greater wisdom and power than yourself or the enemy.

It is important to follow the path that God has set for your life, obey His voice, and surrender to His will. However, the question is, "How do you know the path that He has for your life? How do you build trust?" Having a relationship with God builds a better understanding of His Word. True worship is a reflection of your relationship with Him. Your praise is a mirror image of your prayer life and shows forth your desire to get to know God. All believers can develop and grow in their knowledge and relationship with Him.

A lack of trust shows a lack of intimacy or relationship. That absence of connection reflects a deficiency in your praise and worship. In fact, the limits on your praise in actuality show a lack of interaction between you and God. Suffice to say, the enemy uses this absence of communication to manipulate your condition and play with your mind. The enemy often comes when you are trying to do the right thing. The adversary targets you in every area of your life, so if you are not communicating with God, that inevitably becomes a doorway for the enemy to gain entry.

Let me tell you this: I will praise Him with gratitude. I want to show you why I say praise Him while waiting. I want to demonstrate to you the power you invoke with your praise. I endeavor to stir up your pure mind, inspiring you to remember the gift within you. What should you expect while you are waiting? Consider all the great things God has done in your life and in the lives of others. Jehoshaphat said to the people, "…Hear me, O Judah, and ye inhabitants of Jerusalem; Believe in the LORD your God, so shall ye be established; believe in His prophets, so shall ye prosper," (2 Chr. 20:20).

When they began to sing and to praise the Lord; the Lord set up an ambush against their enemies. When they came towards the watchtower, they looked and there were dead bodies fallen to the Earth; and Jehoshaphat and his people came to take the spoil and they found among the riches, precious jewels, more than they can carry. It took three days to gather all the spoil.

As in this example, the right praise will get God's attention. I will bless the Lord at all times; His praise shall continually be in my mouth. Oh, magnify the Lord with me. Let us exalt His name together. I sought the Lord and He heard me and delivered me from all my fears. Oh, taste and see that the Lord is good! They that seek Him will lack no good thing.

God gave us a Word and He promised that when we offer Him praise and glorify His name, that He will restore our joy and salvation. He upholds us with His free spirit. Thus, I will bless Him while I live; I will lift up my hands in His name. I shall praise Him with joyful lips. I will remember the Lord upon my bed and meditate on thee in the night. Continue to serve the Lord with gladness, come before His presence with singing and bless His name. Oh, that men would praise the Lord for His goodness, and for all the wonderful works that He has shown towards us.

I will praise God; for I am fearfully and wonderfully made. Praise the Lord because He is good. It is good to sing praise to our God, for it is pleasant and praise is comely. Both young men, old men, women and children. Let them praise the name of the Lord for His name alone is excellent. Praise ye the Lord. Praise God in the sanctuary; praise Him in the firament of His power. Praise Him for His mighty acts and according to His excellent greatness. Praise Him with the sound of the trumpet, with the psaltery and harp. Praise Him with the timbrel and in a dance; even the stringed instruments and organs. Praise Him upon the loud cymbals. Let everything that has breath praise the Lord. Keep speaking to yourselves in psalms and hymns and spiritual songs. Make a melody in your heart to the Lord, giving thanks always for all things unto God and the Father, in the name of our Lord Jesus Christ (Ps. 150:1-6).

While you are waiting on your blessings, healing, financial breakthrough and deliverance… praise Him while you wait! Do not be in a hurry, but wait on it. In everything, by prayer and supplication with thanksgiving, let your request be made known unto God. Always rejoice in the Lord, and again I say rejoice. "I feel sick." Rejoice! "I need money." Rejoice! "My kids are acting out." Rejoice! When you have done all that you know to do, stand! I will keep saying it over and over until it sinks in your spirit; praise Him while you wait! No matter what your struggle may be; keep a praise on your lips and in your heart. No matter what things may look like, say, "I'm going to praise Him while I wait!" Let the peace of God rule in your hearts and be thankful. Let the Word of God dwell in you richly, in all wisdom and teaching and admonishing of one another with spiritual songs. Through your many trials, though you may feel overwhelmed, remind yourself that *this* needed to take place.

You may say, "Dr. Brenda, why do you say I need this?" Every trial takes us to another level in God. Behind every struggle, there is a blessing. This is why I encourage you to praise Him through your storms and while you are expecting Him to deliver you, give Him praise! One day you will look back and say, "I see why I had to go through these manifold temptations. Thanks be to God which giveth us the victory through our Lord and Savior." In my case, I didn't understand this principle until God showed me firsthand. He told me, "Be steadfast, unmovable, and while you are waiting, praise Me! For, I am going to open a great door; an effectual door is being opened for you but it does not come without many adversaries." Therefore, while I live, I will praise the Lord. I will sing with a grateful heart.

I will sing praise to God while I have my being. Be happy in the midst of your trial because your hope is in the God of Jacob.

Every day I will bless Him and worship Him forever. I will speak of His glory and talk of His power. God upholds all that fall, raising up those that are bowed down. All that wait on Him, He gives their meat in due season. He will fulfill the desire of them that fear Him and put their trust in Him. God keeps and covers all those that love Him. He opens His hands and satisfies the Godly desires of those who are upright. How can you *not* praise Him while you wait?

Every day God is giving me strength; He teaches me how to fight in this war and win. He is my goodness, my fortress, my high tower, my deliverer, my shield; in whom I put my trust. I thank God who always counsels me and causes me to triumph in every place. I must praise Him! God has given all of us the power to be overcome every setback. Therefore, my faith is in Him.

Do not let anyone take or stop your praise, for that is your crown. In order to see Jesus, you have to be an overcomer. **Walk with a victorious mindset; it's already done**! God gave us a word, in Him we can inherit all things. Isn't that a reason to give Him glory? The Lord is a sun and a shield, it is He who gives grace and glory. No good thing will He withold from those who are righteous. He will give us what is good and our land shall increase. That is why, I am going to keep praising Him while I wait. The joy of the Lord is my strength. I feel a praise in my heart and a dance in my feet! Glory to God! Glory to the King of Kings and the Lord of Lords. He is our bread in a dry and thirsty land. He will cause you to reap what you have sown.

The God of all grace, who called us unto His eternal glory by Christ Jesus, will bless you after you have suffered awhile. Don't miss this because it is powerful! When you have been through the storms and the rain and can still continue to praise Him, anyhow; God will make you perfect. He will establish you, strengthen you and settle you. In that alone, you should start thanking God and giving Him glory! Now, you know why you have been through so much 'hell'. Yes, Christ suffered, therefore; we have to suffer with Him. However, thanks be to God that you do not have to keep on suffering! He cares for you. You can come out through your praise (1 Pet. 5:6-10).

God revealed to me something that blessed me so much. I want to share it with you, I call it my "Praise Revelation." Catch hold of the word and I hope it blesses you just like it blessed me! One day, I was going through so badly. I mean, it was intense. I needed money for church bills, personal bills and I needed a new house. At the time, I didn't know everything God had in store for me through my praise and trusting Him. In addition to the bills, I had lumps in both breasts and the doctors wanted me to undergo surgery. Some years prior, my sister had her breasts removed after being diagnosed with breast cancer. They found the same lumps in my daughter and if that was not enough; I was told, "We also see something abnormal in your abdomen." God, what could happen next? I thought to myself: "How can I be happy and give you praise God when all these negative things are happening in my life? How much more can I take?"

The trials continued; back to back. One of my grandsons started hemorrhaging from his nostrils and the doctors reported their might be problems on his brain. "My God, he's only fifteen years old!"

I needed to hear a Word from God! This was a lot to take on at one time and I did not want to lose hope. I cried out to God in my distress and pleaded for relief in the midst of uncertainty.

When we, instead of feeling hopeless and becoming discouraged, choose to render praise to God in the midst of challenging circumstances or difficulties that arise, we actually activate His divine power to step in and help us. Praise becomes a powerful weapon or tool to push back and defeat the adversary. Our weapons are not Earthly; but it is through God that we are fortified and protected against attack.

The Bible says that no weapon formed against the righteous shall prosper. "No weapon that is formed against thee shall prosper; and every tongue that shall rise against thee in judgment thou shalt condemn. This is the heritage of the servants of the Lord, and their righteousness is of me, saith the Lord," (Isa. 54:17).

It also says in Ephesians:

> *"Finally, my brethren, be strong in the Lord, and in the power of His might. Put on the whole armour of God, that ye may be able to stand against the wiles of the devil. For we wrestle not against flesh and blood, but against principalities, against powers, against the rulers of the darkness of this world, against spiritual wickedness in high places. Wherefore take unto you the whole armour of God, that ye may be able to withstand in the evil day, and having done all, to stand. Stand therefore, having your loins girt about with truth, and having on the breastplate of righteousness; And your feet shod with the preparation of the gospel of peace; Above all, taking the shield of faith, wherewith ye shall be able to quench all the fiery darts of the wicked. And take the helmet of salvation, and the sword of the Spirit, which is the Word of God: Praying always with all prayer and supplication in the Spirit, and watching thereunto with all perseverance and supplication for all saints,"* (Eph. 6:10-18).

So, remember, despite what trials and tribulations may have transpired in your life and past; regardless of any unexpected occurrences that happen during the course of the day, keep a reverence for God in your heart and on your lips. There is power in your praise, in your faith, and in the Word of God! Did you know the word 'praise' appears 248 times in the King James translation of the Bible? It is up to you to explore the deeper meaning and significance of it being mentioned that many number of times. Still, one thing is for sure; God is magnified through the expression of your countenance, the exhortation of your speech, and the surrendering of your hands. Praising God means to resist the enemy within (your own selfish desires) and the enemy that is out.

God spoke to me in the midst of my trials and He said to me, "Brenda, your blessings are in your praise." In everything I was going through, as if that was not enough, the medical reports continued to fight against me. The doctor said the left side of my body was deteriorating and that is why I was experiencing acute pain. According to their report, as a result of the changes, my left side was uneven with my right side.

Sometimes, the enemy seeks to overwhelm the saints and contrary thoughts flood the mind, "How can I overcome all of this? It is too much to bear!" In the middle of everything I was facing, God spoke again, "I told you your miracle is in your praise! It is in your praise!" I knew I had to put my trust in God and praise Him like I had never praised Him before. I chose to believe the report of the Lord which says, I am healed, delivered, and set free. His report says, "By His stripes I was healed." That's past tense; not trying to be or going to be, but the Scripture is a declaration that it is already done. I AM healed!"

The Lord said, "Tell the people it's in their praise! Then, He took me to Psalm 67:1-7. God be merciful to us and bless us. Cause your face to shine upon us; that your way may be known in the Earth. Your saving health among all nations. Let the people praise you, O God; let all the people praise thee. Let the nations be glad and sing for joy, you will judge the people righteously. You are the one who governs the nations upon the Earth. Let the people praise thee. Then, shall the Earth yield her increase. Then, the land will give us a harvest and God- you will bless us. God will bless and increase us; and all the ends of the Earth shall fear Him.

Praising God requires humility. When you are sincere in your praise, you are not paying attention to those around you, the tempo of the music, or the lighting. You're not trying to be cute or stuffy behind various so-called "titles". You don't stop praising Him because the music stops. You don't change the tempo of your step because the beat of the drum may have changed. A sincere praise will have you looking "ugly" sometimes. Some of you know what exactly what I am talking about here. Your left shoe might be behind one pew and the other might still be on your foot. A sincere worshipper will still honor and embrace His presence, even when there is no sound, no lighting, no choir director, or praise team. A true worshipper drops to their knees and prays to their Sovereign God with tears streaming down their face. They jump up and down and shout with gratefulness! Their praise cannot be contained.

"Lift up your hands in the sanctuary, and bless the Lord," (Ps. 134:2).

One has to be willing to surrender, give up control, and release their whole being to God. It requires an abandonment of self and clearing the mind from the cares of this world. This may not be an easy thing to do because maybe you have been dealing with so much and the pressures of the world have been weighing you down. Perhaps, your mind seems to continue to be bombarded with thoughts of financial obligations, children, relationships, job problems, and other worries. Things might be difficult right now, but let me tell you this; your praise is the key to victory over worry, insecurity, doubt, fear, and burdens. Although it may seem hard to do, I am encouraging you to rejoice and relax in the presence of an omnipotent and mighty King! You must, not maybe, but you must relinquish your worries to God and release every stronghold that seeks to keep your life in bondage. However, this is done through the power of praise. It is through praise and honor to God, that we can all be free. Stand to your feet and praise the Lord!

God is the God of MORE! He is more than enough, more than any situation, more than any fear, more than any disease. He is limitless and His power is unfathomable. God is able to do exceedingly and abundantly above our greatest expectation. Take the limits off of God in each area of your life and watch His will for your life be revealed. Take the limits off and know that the impossible is possible with Him! He is a wise master builder; we are like clay being struck, formed, and shaped into His supreme desire for our life.

Understand that suffering is a fixed pattern to promote the mission of Christ, and to bring glory to His name. God's imagination is creative and ingenious. He is boundless and limitless. He is clever; inventive in all of His ways and methods He chooses to bless us. The power of God is exceptional. Yet, in order for it to be fruitful in our lives, we must trust Him to bring us through our circumstances and to help us release every stronghold therein.

When you cry out to God and surrender to Him, it ignites something in the atmosphere. It kindles a fire within your soul! The enemy, then begins to back up. Through your confession and positive decision-making, you become free. When you turn to God and praise Him, the fire of God consumes you. It saturates the atmosphere and spreads. From one person to the next, the fire of God is burning away everything that is not like Him and setting His people free. Deliverance is in God's mighty hands. Prosperity is in God's mighty hands. Peace is in God's mighty hands. Joy is in God's mighty hands.

When your soul is kindled in worship, all of Heaven takes notice. There is a surreal feeling of tranquility and rest in Him. God is a consuming fire, in Him; the devil has no choice but to flee. "For our God is a consuming fire," (Heb. 12:29). Loose that fire within through exhortation to God.

Daniel states:

> *"He answered and said, Lo, I see four men loose, walking in the midst of the fire, and they have no hurt; and the form of the fourth is like the Son of God. Then Nebuchadnezzar came near to the mouth of the burning fiery furnace, and spake, and said, Shadrach, Meshach, and Abednego, ye servants of the most High God, come forth, and come hither. Then Shadrach, Meshach, and Abednego, came forth of the midst of the fire. And the princes, governors, and captains, and the king's counsellors, being gathered together, saw these men, upon whose bodies the fire had no power, nor was an hair of their head singed, neither were their coats changed, nor the smell of fire had passed on them. Then Nebuchadnezzar spake, and said, Blessed be the God of Shadrach, Meshach, and Abednego, who hath sent his angel, and delivered his servants that trusted in Him, and have changed the king's word, and yielded their bodies, that they might not serve nor worship any god, except their own God. Therefore I make a decree, That every people, nation, and language, which speak any thing amiss against the God of Shadrach, Meshach, and Abednego, shall be cut in pieces, and their houses shall be made a dunghill: because there is no other God that can deliver after this sort,"* (Dan. 3:25-29).

Praise ye the Lord! Be a worshipper, not a worrier!

You see, worry is a negative emotion that paralyzes the worrier. Worry causes a person to become anxious and uneasy. It causes a person to focus on their difficulties and troubles. Worry is fear and as the saying goes, "Fear is false evidence appearing real." When a believer is worried or fearful, God cannot have ultimate control over your life. Fear is an inability to trust God. It causes a ripple effect of frustration and depression in the life of a believer.

Take time out and read Psalm 66:1-16.

Everything you have been praying and seeking God for can be found in your praise! Take back your joy that the devil stole from you. I did just that. The joy of the Lord IS your strength. Make a joyful noise to God, everybody in every land. Sing for the honor of His name. Make His praise glorious. Give God back His Word! Remind Him of His promises, saying, "God, I know that you are a healer. You have all the riches and everything that I need is in you!" Through the greatness of His power, miracles happen! It is true that sickness, money, worry, and everything else have to submit to Him. Only He can do great and terrible things! I heard the Lord saying unto me, "All the Earth shall worship Him and that means you too, Brenda. Didn't I turn the sea into dry land? Didn't they go through the flood on foot? Didn't they rejoice in me? Am I your King and your Lord? Is there anything too hard for me? Have I really, ever failed you?

In me, all things are possible." Then, I responded, "No, Lord. You have never failed me."

Imagine! Think on how powerful God is. He has made the Heaven and the Earth by His great power and His stretched out arm. He is the God of all flesh, there is nothing too hard for Him (Jer. 32:17, 27). Sarah thought it was impossible to have a son in her old age, God calmed her fears and reminded her of His power (Gen. 18:10).

He ruleth by His power, forever and ever. His eyes see everything. His eyes are over the entire nation and with Him all things are possible (Mrk. 10:27). Surely, God can see my needs. Then He said, O bless our God, ye people, and make the voice of His praise to be heard. He holds our soul in His hand and suffers our feet not to be moved.

Praise confuses the enemy. When you praise God, out of the ordinary things will begin to happen. If your heart is right, He will bless you beyond anything you can ask or think. His Word does not return void. If He said it, He is faithful and just to bring it to pass. God declares that when His Word goes out, it will not return void. It prospers wherever He sends it (Isa. 55:10-11). You must have faith; without it you cannot please Him (Heb. 11:6; Mrk. 11:22). We have to show God that we believe Him, through our praise. The Word says, "Faith without works is dead." Is your faith alive today? Prove it by praising Him in advance for what you need. In praising Him, do not waiver (Jas. 1:8-12). Praise God with a pure heart and believe that IT is done.

Praise and Deliverance – Deliverance is in your praise. We live in a world where many people praise God for personal gain. They look at God for what He can do for them today. They praise Him for a new car, house, job, a new husband or wife, but what about praising Him because of who He IS? We should give Him praise and thanks for all things. Praise God not only for the things He gives us, but for the life He allows us to live. The Bible says in Psalm 100:3, "Know ye that the Lord He is God; it is He that hath made us, and not ourselves; we are His people, and the sheep of His pasture."

We should give God praise for who He is and not so much for what He can do for us. We should give praise to God for those delivered from drugs and alcohol. We should give Him praise for setting us free from all our sins and giving us another chance. Worship Him for sending His only begotten Son, Jesus Christ, to die on the cross for sinners like me and you. Give God the praise for waking us up in the morning to see another day. Give God the praise for delivering our family and friends. We need to praise God because we love Him and we are thankful. "I will bless the Lord at all times: His praise shall continually be in my mouth," (Ps. 34:1).

Once again, it does not matter what the circumstances in our lives may be, whether all is well or if everything is falling apart; we are still to give God the praise. Praise Him while you wait! In order to give God the praise that He truly deserves our hearts need to be right and our minds must be clear. Only those who love God will be able to give Him true praise and worship because they know who they are in Christ Jesus. The Bible says in John 4:24, that God is a Spirit and they that worship Him must worship Him in spirit and in truth.

Learn how to praise God. It's not hard. Just think of all the things that He has done for you. Think about all those trials and tribulations that God has brought you through. Think about how you once lived versus the way that you live now. I can guarantee that if your heart is right, you will start to give God the praise that He truly deserves.

We can take some direction from Job. In Scripture, Job did not go back from the commandment of God. Job stood. He held his feet, and his steps were kept. He didn't decline. He esteemed the words of his mouth more than his necessary food. He said, "When I went out to the gate through the city, when I prepared my seat in the street! The young men saw me, and hid themselves, and the aged arose and stood up. The princes refrained talking, and laid their hand on their mouth. The nobles held their peace, and their tongue cleaved to the roof of their mouth. When the ear heard me, then it blessed me; and when the eye saw me, it gave witness to me: Because I delivered the poor that cried, and fatherless, and him that had none to help him," (Job 29:7-12).

Job carried a blessing with him because of his words and his praise towards God. He continued in faith, trusting God, and standing on his praise. He praised Him while waiting! Job believed God would never leave him nor forsake him. He had a made up mind that he was going to wait until his change came. When you are trusting God for your deliverance, you have to have a made up mind and possess faith. No matter what you see or hear, you have to know that help is on the way. As a matter of fact, it is already done!

We give others strength when they hear our testimony and our faith towards God. Also, when we stand in what we believe, it touches the heart of others. Job believed in the word which God had given him. He knew that God was going to bless him and give him more than what he had from the beginning. When he was ready to perish, his blessings caused the widows heart to sing for joy. You have to sing for joy! Job became eyes to the blind and feet to the lame. He put on righteousness and it clothed him.

We should be like Job when he opened his mouth; men gave ear and waited for his counsel because he had the words of the

Lord. His speech was like rain coming down in a dry and thirsty land. They waited and opened their mouths to the sky for rain drops, for the latter rain.

When the morning stars sang together, all the Sons of God shouted for joy (Job 38:7). Job was sure not to let his friend's words of doubt and unbelief cause him to waiver. He believed the words which God had spoken to him. He didn't let his faith fail and stood on the promises of God. He was continuously strong in his faith; not giving heed to doubtful tongues.

God will allow things to happen in our lives to prove us. When we endure, trust, and continue in our praise to Him; we can praise our way right out of whatever is bothering us. When God tries us, He tries us as silver is tried. I can testify that I have gone through the fire and the flood, but I never stopped giving God the praise. I knew He was going to bring me through. He says in Psalm 67:6 that after we praise, "Then shall the Earth yields her increase, and God, even our own God shall bless us."

Your increase can be found in your praise and worship. I started praising God and telling others who were in the midst of the fire to praise Him too. My soul cries out 'Hallelujah' every time I think about where the Lord has brought me from and how He saved me from the hand of death. I learned to leave the Earth and reach the Heavens in my praise. I left everything behind: circumstances, troubles, and pain. I let my mind forget what was happening on the Earth and enter into a Heavenly place of praise and worship. As I entered into this Heavenly place, I found pure and true praise to God. Ask God to refresh and renew you in His Word. This is a new day. Then, God birthed a new song in my heart, "A Time of Refreshing."

In order for you to be refreshed and enter into your Heavenly place of peace. Your praise must be released as a weapon against every stronghold. Use the power of praise to defeat the enemy and to move him out of your way, so that you may reach your goal. Overcome your obstacles to achieve your dreams. It's in your praise!

WORDS OF EMPOWERMENT

1. **Song: Time of Refreshing (Dr. Brenda Jefferson)**
   It's time for refreshing! I've got joy, I've got peace, this is a new day, this is a new year. It's time! This is a new me, I've got a new mind, a new thought, and a new praise. Rejoice in the Lord always and again I say, rejoice! Just state it! Claim it! Believe it! It's time for a refreshing.

2. It doesn't matter what you are going through, how you feel or what things look like. He said, "Oh clap your hands all ye people. Shout unto God with a voice of

triumph," (Ps. 47:1). While you are waiting on God, praise Him. There will be battles and trials in your life but never stop giving Him worship. Think yourself happy through it all! When you praise Him, know why you are praising Him. A good thing to remember, is that the battle is already won, so you can go ahead and shout NOW! He has done it! Sing praises to our God and King. Sing praises to His name.

3. **Song: O Clap your Hands (Dr. Brenda Jefferson)**
   O clap your hands, all ye people. Shout unto God with a voice of triumph! O clap your hands, all ye people. Shout unto God with a voice of triumph! After all that He has done for me, He gave His life to set me free. That is why I celebrate His name, clapping my hands just to give Him praise. O clap your hands, all ye people, shout unto God with a voice of triumph! Make a joyful noise unto God, all ye lands. Sing for the honor of His name. Make His praises glorious. Anybody, anybody, anybody? Anybody, anybody, everybody? Come on clap your hands! Come on clap your hands!

4. This is the confidence that I will make with them after those trials, says the Lord. I will put my laws in their

hearts and in their minds and I will write them. Their fears and iniquities, I will remember no more. Be bold and enter into Holiness by the blood of Jesus. Let us draw near with a true heart, a full assurance of faith, having our hearts sprinkled from an evil conscience and our bodies washed with pure water. Let us hold fast the profession of our faith, without wavering (for He is faithful that promised). Call to remembrance the former days, in which, after you were illuminated. You endured a great fight of affliction! You were gazed upon by others in your reproach and afflictions, and took joyfully the spoiling of your goods. Know that you have in Heaven, better and enduring substance.

5. Cast not away your confidence. It has great recompense of reward. You have need of patience, after you have done the will of God, that you might receive the promise. The just will live by faith, but if any man draws back, my soul has no pleasure in him (Heb. 10:32-38).

6. Give and it shall be given unto you, good measure, pressed down, shaken together and running over shall men give unto your bosom. Job gave the Word of God and stood still in his praise, until God moved. God gave

Job back double for all his trouble. He blessed his latter end more than his beginning. Bless God and make His voice to be heard.

7. God has to prove us and try us. He laid afflictions upon us and caused men to ride over our heads. We went through fire and water, but God brought us out. When we came out, we were in a wealthy place. Praise the name of the Lord! Glory to the Most High!

8. Everything you need is in your praise, therefore, do not draw back. Do not allow your flesh to dictate your flow in worship. Release your heart in worship. Allow your hands to magnify the Lord. Give permission to your voice to utter salutations to God. Clap your hands and rejoice in Him. Bless His name. Sing forth His praise, dance and enjoy the Lord. Fellowship with Him in worship.

9. We believe in the power of praise. Chains are broken; the captives are set free. The lame can walk and miracles happen in the midst of your praise. Your faith and trust in God will take you places which seem impossible to man, but with God the impossible is made possible

(Heb. 11:1,6). Wait on the Lord and be of good courage. He will strengthen your heart (Ps. 27:14). Cast every care upon Him. Why? Because He cares for you (1 Pet. 5:7). Praise Him for His mighty acts (Ps. 150:2). Be sober, be vigilant. Your adversary roams about as a roaring lion (He's not, He just appears to be). This adversary is seeking those he may devour. Watch and pray!

10. Praise the name of the Lord; for He is worthy to be praised. That is why I seek Him and give Him honor, in the morning and in the afternoon. I will praise Him all the day long. When you communicate and share the Word of God, He blesses you. The Word of God gives you power and strength. People are watching you, so be the light that invokes others to give God praise. You may be the only Jesus some people will ever see. You were once in darkness, yet now you are a light to the world. Walk as children of the light. Remember, the fruit of the Spirit is in all goodness and righteousness. Redeem your time and be wise. Understand what the will of the Lord is for your life. Give thanks, always. You have to stir up the gifts which are in you, the Holy Spirit of God. Hold fast to what you have been taught. Hold fast to His faithful Word that you may be able, by sound doctrine, to exhort and persuade the nay-sayers.

COURSE TWO DAILY AFFIRMATIONS

- I praise and thank God that He has given me His Word. I place His Word as a defensive barrier against anything that is contrary to these beliefs.
- I will thank God for giving me a pure and true praise.
- I do not have to be prompted and primed to give God praise.
- My praise is a lifestyle. I will give Him praise all the day long.
- When I come into His presence, I am saturated in the Word. I am able to pour out of the depth of my heart how much I love Him.
- He knows me personally and God lives in my praise.
- I am thankful that He commanded me to teach others how to come into His presence to worship with a clean heart.
- I will lift up my hands in the sanctuary and in remembrance of who He is. I will remember where He has brought me from.
- I WILL PRAISE HIM WHILE I WAIT!

Study Scriptures to Strengthen You

Deuteronomy 8:10

1 Samuel 2:1

1 Samuel 12:24

2 Chronicles 20

2 Chronicles 32:7-8

Psalm 5:2-3; 34:1-5,7,10

Psalm 51:15; 63:1-7

Psalm 84:1-12; 85:12

Psalm 100:1-4; 107:8; 130:5

Psalm 139:14; 144:1-2

Psalm 145:2, 10-21

Psalm 146:2-5; 147:1, 5-6

Psalm 145:15; 149:3

Psalm 148:12-13; 150:1-6

Ephesians 5:18-20

Philippians 4:4-6

Colossians 3:15-17

1 Peter 1:6-9

2 Peter 1:3-4

1 Corinthians 15:57-58; 16:9

2 Corinthians 9:6-8; 2:14

1 John 5:4

Revelations 3:5, 11-13, 18-22

Revelations 21:5-8

Isaiah 58:11

Study Scriptures to Strengthen You

Matthew 6:30-34

Romans 8:25

Job 14:14

James 5:10-11

Acts 26:2

St. John 4:23

Course 3

Remove Ungodly Strongholds

"For though we walk in the flesh, we do not war after the flesh: for the weapons of our warfare are not carnal, but mighty through God to the pulling down of strongholds; Casting down imaginations, and every high thing that exalteth itself against the knowledge of God, and bringing into captivity every thought to the obedience of Christ," (2 Cor. 10:3-5).

"The Lord is good, a strong hold in the day of trouble; and He knoweth them that trust in Him," (Nah. 1:7).

In Course One, we discussed the reason why struggles exist and the importance of moving over, to allow God to take the helm, so that we can navigate the storms of life safely. We discussed the importance of dropping our anchor and remaining sure, steadfast, and steady. In Course Two, we went in depth about praising God while you wait and touched on the power of praise. As we continue into this next course, I would like for you to consider the power of strongholds and how they impact your life. What is hindering or preventing you from being your absolute best? Discover new things about yourself, as we learn about the principle of Course Three: *Removing Ungodly Strongholds.*

Once you begin to live for Christ, you become a threat to the enemy. You have to put on the whole armor of God and "be strong in the Lord and in the power of His might," so that you can withstand any attack from our adversary. You are made free in Christ and the Bible teaches that no one can come in and take away what God has given you unless he binds you (Matt.12:29).

In order to do this the enemy seeks to kill, steal, and destroy all that is good in your life. He wants to bind you! He wants to kill the love and unity; steal your joy, peace, and happiness; and destroy your marriage, family, and life. Our adversary goes to war with anything that produces love, unity, and obedience to God's way. He attempts to entangle and enslave through fleshly lusts with the aim of causing you to lose your inheritance. He sets up these strongholds to cause you to lose hope and fail. Yet, as I have said before, God can do anything but fail (1 Pet. 5:7-8).

A *stronghold* is defined as "a fortress or place where a particular cause or belief is strongly defended or upheld." It is "a place that has been fortified so as to protect it against attack." When we talk about strongholds, there are two types: *Godly and ungodly strongholds.* **Ungodly strongholds** are those causes and beliefs that are vigorously defended and upheld, even when they are contrary to God's will and His way. Often, these are evil thoughts or ungodly behaviors that you cannot seem to overcome. A **Godly stronghold** is a place or space of refuge that is reinforced to increase its effectiveness and provides the necessary protection to withstand any attack that comes against it.

The Bible teaches us about being bold in our faith, "For God hath not given us the spirit of fear; but of power, and of love, and of a sound mind," (2 Tim. 1:7). It also teaches us that we don't battle against flesh and blood, but rather against principalities, powers, rulers of the darkness of this world, and against spiritual wickedness in high places (Eph. 6:12). These plots and wicked maneuverings of the enemy establish strongholds which can wreak havoc in a person's life. These strongholds by the enemy are designed to destroy anything that

God has ordained and has in cases destroyed marriages, families, and lives.

"Beware lest any man spoil you through philosophy and vain deceit, after the tradition of men, after the rudiments of the world, and not after Christ. For in Him dwelleth all the fullness of the Godhead bodily. And ye are complete in Him, which is the head of all principality and power," (Col. 2:8-10).

Despite the attempts of Satan, God is the rock of our salvation. Trust in Him, take Him as your shield and your refuge. He is your Savior and will save you from harm (2 Sam. 22:3). The enemy of God tempts you in every place and situation. Beware! He aligns ungodly strongholds which are constructed on sexual immorality, uncleanness, excessive indulgence in sensual pleasures, idolatry, hatred, contention, variance, and discord.

Even more, he seeks to cause division, envy and jealousy, selfish ambition, he wants you to entertain dark magic, drunkenness, and more. These characteristics or activities are contrary to the Spirit of God and produce lies, secrets, hiding, and fear. Other wicked temptations can cause a lack of openness and transparency, arrogance, stubbornness, confusion, anger, hatred, guilt, shame, bickering, arguing, strife, distrust, division, and many other unsightly characteristics in God's eyes. It is important to take refuge in God because the enemy walks about seeking whom he may devour (1 Pet. 5:8).

While you may be tempted in your life by things that have tempted many before you, God will not allow you to be overtaken or suffer a burden above your ability to handle. God is faithful and always provides a way for you to escape temptation (1 Cor. 10:13).

When you are in trouble, cry out to God. "The Lord also will be a refuge for the oppressed, a refuge in times of trouble," (Ps. 9:9). When you seek refuge in the Most High, He will tear down every ungodly stronghold. "And the fortress of the high fort of thy walls shall He bring down, lay low, and bring to the ground, even to the dust," (Isa. 25:12).

What a mighty God we serve! In tearing down these walls of unrighteousness, as shown above, He removes the strongholds that the enemy uses to enslave in sin. You must operate in truth, love, light, and courage as you pray for protection. Don't give the enemy a hiding place or a way in. His methods are contentious and deceptive, but God's way is truth and love. When you are temperate, you are able to remain sober-minded not being overcome by emotion and fear. This way you are able to see things clearly. Recognize the cause of your frustration and restore your joy by thinking yourself happy. "A merry heart maketh a cheerful countenance: but by sorrow of the heart the spirit is broken," (Prov. 15:13).

When you are going through your trials and your heart is heavy, you have to remain prayerful, praising God and remembering the promise. If you are only focused on your problems and your own pain, you may miss the lesson in your trial. If you are all caught up in your sorrow and having a "pity party," what you are in essence saying is that God is not able to bring you out. You have to possess a merry heart because the Word says, "…he that is of a merry heart hath a continual feast," (Prov. 15:15).

Regardless of what is going on in your life, God is able! Therefore, in knowing that to be the truth, there is no reason to mourn over the tactics of the enemy. Now, this doesn't mean that you don't talk about what you need to in order to achieve resolution, it simply means that you don't have to lose your joy over the situation.

Remember that God is a deliverer. When you are going through, simply open your mouth to say, "I AM Happy!" Open your mouth and declare you are blessed! "A man hath joy by the answer of his mouth: and a word spoken in due season, how good is it!" (Prov. 15:23).

Don't just release your worries, cast every care that you have on God. He cares for you and He will be your fortress. Stand firm in faith and truth. God will tear down every ungodly stronghold. All things are possible in Christ. You are free in Him and God makes the impossible possible.

Let go of your fears. Even if your marriage seems like it is in a state of disrepair, believe God can make the impossible possible. Tear down the stronghold of division, disharmony, and contention. Tear down the stronghold of impatience, not feeling worthy, or ungratefulness. A lack of appreciation, giving too much of yourself, self-abuse or feeling like you have to be everything to everybody is a stronghold. Tear it down! These strongholds can prevent you from being yourself, prevent you from building a relationship with God, cultivating your gifts and talents, or appreciating who God has placed in your life. Be committed to tear down every stronghold in your life!

If you are going through it, know that others in the body of Christ are going through it too; but God is a deliverer and makes the impossible possible! God is not limited or confined. He is able to free you from trouble and empower you to achieve your dream.

Make your requests known and petition God for what you want. Believe in your dreams. There are infinite amount of opportunities provided by God for divine overflow when you seek Him. Don't try to restrict God. Don't doubt Him and don't limit His power. Remove all ungodly strongholds. Limit any negative conversations that contradict what you are trying to achieve.

Statements of Doubt can include:

- "God, I want you to bless me with a car, *but*. . ."
- "God, I need a husband or wife, *but* they must meet these criteria. . ."
- "Lord, I need you to deliver my children, *but* do it this way. . ."
- "Lord, I need you to heal my body, *but* the doctor says that it is. . ."
- "God, I know I don't thank you enough, *but* today I'm tired. I only want to clap my hands. . ."

It is the "*but*" that demonstrates a lack of trust in God and confirms doubt in His ability to "make it alright." It is the "but" that gives an indication of an ungodly stronghold. When you limit God, you create boundaries around His power and consequently restrict the measure of His blessings in your life. I keep saying and I will continue to say, God can do anything but fail. There are no limitations to what He can do. Remove the stronghold of doubt. Remove the shackles off your mind which confine and limit God in your life.

Yes, you might be fed up with the struggles, the obstacles, the trials, but think yourself happy. "I think myself happy, king Agrippa, because I shall answer for myself this day before thee touching all the things whereof I am accused of the Jews," (Acts 26:2).

You've got to think yourself happy, no matter what things look like, no matter what comes against you. Say: "I'm happy." Keep praising God and keep pleasing God, even in the midst of the trials. As my husband, the Bishop says, you shouldn't look for God in just one way; you have to look for Him in all directions. He makes uncommon moves and does things out of the norm. God knows what is best for you and while you may want it one way, God may find you *need* it another way. Tear down all ungodly strongholds!

There is nothing wrong with being specific with your prayers. As a matter of fact, you should be very decisive with what you are asking for, then expect that God can and will deliver. Still, this is where trust comes in. You have to trust God—trust that He loves you and can see further than you can see. You have to trust that God is all-knowing and can prevent valleys, heartache, trials, and trouble through His wisdom. "For my thoughts are not your thoughts, neither are your ways my ways, saith the Lord. For as the Heavens are higher than the

Earth, so are my ways higher than your ways, and my thoughts than your thoughts," (Isa. 55:8-9).

The enemy comes when you are trying to do the right thing and targets every area in your life. He tempts you in moments of weakness. "Wherefore take unto you the whole armour of God, that ye may be able to withstand in the evil day, and having done all, to stand," (Eph. 6:13).

The Bible does not say "[if] the enemy comes in like a flood…" It says, "…*When* the enemy shall come in like a flood, the Spirit of the Lord shall lift up a standard against him," (Isa. 59:19). In this context, a *standard* is "a level of quality or attainment." In other words, the Lord will raise you up or increase the quality in your life. Likewise, quality is "the standard of something as measured against other things; it is the degree of excellence of something; a distinctive attribute or characteristic possessed by someone or something." How can you know the excellence of God and His ability to raise you up to a higher position or level than your enemy? You have to seek refuge in Him and in His Word!

The Bible says in 2 Corinthians 10:3-4, "For though we walk in the flesh, we do not war after the flesh: For the weapons of our warfare are not carnal, but mighty through God to the pulling down of strongholds."

It further goes on to say, "Casting down imaginations, and every high thing that exalteth itself against the knowledge of God, and bringing into captivity every thought to the obedience of Christ," (2 Cor. 10:5).

Scripture tells us to try every spirit and God will let you know which spirit is of Him. "We are of God: he that knoweth God heareth us; he that is not of God heareth not us. Hereby know we the spirit of truth, and the spirit of error. Beloved, let us love one another: for love is of God; and every one that loveth is born of God, and knoweth God. He that loveth not knoweth not God; for God is love," (1 Jn. 4:6-8).

We are called to live life by the Spirit. We are called, into salvation, to be free and not in bondage. We are admonished to not use our freedom to indulge in the flesh, but rather serve one another in love. When we walk in the Spirit, we will not get tripped up by the flesh. There is a saying that you can tell a tree by the fruit it bears. The fruits of the Spirit are love, joy, peace, longsuffering, gentleness, goodness, faith, meekness, and temperance (Gal. 5:22-23).

Those who belong to Christ have crucified the flesh and are not bound by the law. They are led by the Spirit, choosing to live and walk in the Spirit. They trust in God's protection and provision. The Bible says, "No weapon that is formed against thee shall prosper; and every tongue that shall rise against thee in judgment thou shalt condemn. This is the heritage of the servants of the Lord, and their righteousness is of me, saith the Lord," (Isa. 54:17).

Seek refuge in the Most High and know that He is your fortress. "Lift up your hands in the sanctuary, and bless the Lord," (Ps. 134:2).

One has to be willing to surrender, give up control, and release their whole being to God. It requires complete surrender. This may not be an easy thing to do because maybe you have been dealing with so much and the pressures of the world have been weighing you down. Perhaps, your mind seems to flood with thoughts of financial obligations, children, relationships, career, or other worries. Things might be difficult, but let me tell you this; God can remove every stronghold.

"Nay, in all these things we are more than conquerors through Him that loved us. For I am persuaded, that neither death, nor life, nor angels, nor principalities, nor powers, nor things present, nor things to come, Nor height, nor depth, nor any other creature, shall be able to separate us from the love of God, which is in Christ Jesus our Lord," (Rom. 8:37-39). You have victory over every stronghold—worry, doubt, insecurity, fear, etc. Although it may seem hard to do, you must, not maybe, but you must relinquish your worries to God and release every stronghold that seeks to keep your life in bondage.

Victory is obtainable for every believer. Being victorious can mean fulfillment in your career or marriage. Victory can mean prosperity, freedom from addiction, or deliverance from drugs and alcohol. Each individual has a different measure of victory depending on their own personal life circumstance and issues.

Take the limits off of God by surrendering to Him. Limits place us in captivity, but God has the capability to cause the Earth to tremble and the foundation of a prison to be shaken. God has the power to set us free. "And at midnight Paul and Silas prayed, and sang praises unto God: and the prisoners heard them. And suddenly there was a great earthquake, so that the foundations of the prison were shaken: and immediately all the doors were opened, and every one's bands were loosed," (Acts 16:25-26).

Set a fire within your soul and tell God that you want more of Him! The fire refines us and purifies our inner man - from the inside out. It cleanses our heart and renews a right spirit within us. "And I will bring the third part through the fire, and will refine them as silver is refined, and will try them as gold is tried: they shall call on my name, and I will hear them: I will say, It is my people: and they shall say, The Lord is my God," (Zech. 13:9).

WORDS OF EMPOWERMENT

1. No matter what battles are going on around you, don't let that conflict inside of you. Operate in the Spirit, go within because therein lies the greatest victor. "Ye are of God, little children, and have overcome them: because greater is He that is in you, than he that is in the world," (1 Jn. 4:4).

2. Set your affections in defense of the gospel. Just as you would praise and show your affection to a loved one; show God how much He means to you through your worship. Ignite a fire for God; deep within your being, sending a sweet aroma to fill His nostrils. With tears in your eyes as you bow before the altar, you must release yourself and completely let go. Take your praise to a place of peace; a place where you can hear from Heaven clearly, without any distortion or confusion from the noise of 'this world.'

3. Cry out, "Abba Father," the Lord God is worthy to be praised. Especially when you are feeling extremes of emotions (e.g., distress, fear, joy, happiness), continue to

call out to God. "Nay, in all these things we are more than conquerors through Him that loved us," (Rom. 8:37).

4. Break down the walls and barriers you have set in your mind and aggressively defeat the enemy with your praise. Stand firm in your faith.

5. Be sober. Be vigilant. Your adversary the devil, walks around and is seeking whom He may devour (1 Pet. 5:8). Resist him steadfast in faith through your worship to God. As a believer, be bold in your beliefs. We are sent forth as sheep in the midst of wolves, therefore be wise as a serpent and humble as doves (Matt. 10:16).

6. Know the tactics of the enemy. Know that they cannot prevail when you stand on His Word. "In God I will praise His Word, in God I have put my trust; I will not fear what can flesh do unto me," (Ps. 56:4).

7. Fear no devil; God is a supernatural and mighty God who cannot fail you. His Word says, He will never leave you or forsake you. We command every chain to be broken. We exhort the name of the Lord God. Praise

God in the midst of the battle! Don't wait until the storms in your life are over - Shout Now!

8. Take the limits off of God! He has given you power and authority over any stronghold the enemy tries to bind you with. "Behold, I give unto you power to tread on serpents and scorpions, and over all the power of the enemy: and nothing shall by any means hurt you," (Lk. 10:19).

9. Worship God in Spirit and in Truth!

10. Say to God: "Lord, I want more of you. Lord, I need more of your presence. Lord, I need more of your glory."

COURSE THREE DAILY AFFIRMATIONS

- I will experience the fullness of joy, happiness, and great pleasure in the presence of God.
- I acknowledge that God is the great I AM.
- I recognize that God is the Prince of peace.
- I turn to God, as He is the Everlasting Father.
- I bow to God because He is THE King of Glory.
- God is strong and mighty in battle. He is Alpha and Omega.
- I break every chain in my mind through the power of my praise and the Word of God.
- God is boundless and limitless; there is nothing that can confine Him.
- I fully and completely trust God's plan and purpose for my life.
- I surrender to God today and every day. I rest in His covering of protection.

Study Scriptures to Strengthen You

1 Peter 1:8

Psalm 47:1

Psalm 56:4

Psalm 91:1-4

Psalm 110:1-2

John 10:10

2 Chronicles 7:14

1 Peter 5:8

Romans 12:21

Matthew 10:16

Matthew 18:18-19

Joshua 1:9

Joshua 23:10

Isaiah 40:31

1 John 3:8

1 Timothy 6:12

2 Thessalonians 3:3

Zechariah 4

Course 4

The Seed of Righteousness

"Therefore it is of faith, that it might be by grace, to the end the promise might be sure to all the seed; not to that only which is of the law, but to that also which is of the faith of Abraham; who is the father of us all," (Rom. 4:16).

"Let everything that hath breath praise the Lord. Praise ye the Lord," (Ps. 150:6).

In the last course, we discussed how to ignite a fire within us, setting ablaze and destroying anything that is not like God. We spoke on how the enemy uses your mind and your emotions to move you "off your square." He wants to shift you from your position and sift you like wheat. The enemy's job is to remind you of your past experiences and disappointments, to cloud your mind with negative self-chatter. As we continue this walk together, the next topic I would like to highlight is: *The Seed of Righteousness.* This principle guides the sharing in Course Four.

When a seed is planted in the ground, there are no immediate signs of life. There is no visible fruit, there are no roots, and there is no stem to break through the soil. At that moment, it's just an apparent seed lying on the surface waiting to be cultivated. Yet, in order for that seed to germinate, three needs must be met: **water, warmth, and the right environment**. Every seed must have these three things fulfilled, otherwise it will not sprout.

A plant will not grow from out of a seed, until the hard outer shell has been broken. This happens by the right amount of water reaching the tiny embryo within the hard outer coat, causing it to swell and to soften. Once the embryo swells and the outer coat softens, it gives way for the tiny seedling within to break free and come forth.

The first signs of life from the seedling are not readily witnessed until it reaches the surface. The beginning process is still hidden underneath the soil. However, as this tiny plant comes forth, it produces a taproot. A taproot is the first fruit—the central part of the plant or the main vertical root from which lateral roots branch off from. This thick, long root goes deep within the soil and carries nutrients to the plant from deeper sources. At this stage, the plant cannot be witnessed because again, it is hidden behind the veil of darkness (the soil). While obscured from view, the taproot reaches down into the soil in search of water from those deeper sources and a firm resting place to establish a strong foundation for the whole plant. Once the taproot anchors deep within the soil, the underground stem of the plant or seedling stretches upward in search of light. The stem has four distinct functions: 1.) Elevate and support the leaves, flowers, and fruit; 2.) Keep the leaves exposed to the light; 3.) Provide a secure space for the plant to hold its leaves, flowers, and fruit, 4.) Transport fluid between the root and the shoot.

It's important to understand that plants have two organ systems: the root system and the shoot system. The shoot undergirds the stem. So, while the stem has many functions it is actually part of the shoot system along with the leaves, buds, flowers, and fruits. The leaves are the place where the plant's food is produced. The root system and the shoot system are counterparts. However, the roots are below the ground and the shoots are anything above the ground. Yet, they are complementary systems that are interdependent. The shoots absorb nutrients via the roots, and in turn shares that which is received to other parts of the plant system.

Now let's put this into a spiritual context.

There is a time and season for everything in life. The Scripture says in Ecclesiastes 3:1, "To everything there is a season, and a time to every purpose under the Heaven."

As there are seasons for harvest, there are also seasons for planting. During the planting season, the ground must be cultivated to be a good environment, fertile and ready to receive that tiny seed of life. Before a seed is planted into the soil, the ground must be tilled. The soil must be prepared by pulling up weeds and breaking up the hard and crusty soil so that air, water, and nutrients can be absorbed and retained.

In this comparison, the heart can be likened to the soil. Perhaps you have run across a person, who prior to coming to Christ had overwhelming difficulties, constantly struggling to climb a mountain of obstacles. Previously, they may have been overcome by disappointment and therefore show forth a very harsh and cynical disposition in dealing with others. It appears that their heart is filled with and hardened by anger, bitterness, and resentment. They refuse or may not know how to forgive, constantly blaming others for the anguish and pain in their life. No matter what anyone says or does, their thick skin and "tough" exterior is almost impossible to penetrate. Seemingly, no one or anything can break through the walls of pain and hurt deep in their heart.

It is only by planting seeds of charity in such a heart, that a change can happen. Yet, such a heart is unable to receive love until it has been cultivated and it takes a wise farmer or gardener to effectively accomplish such a feat.

To understand this spiritual comparison, we must first understand these three things—**water (the Word), warmth (Holy Spirit & the fruits of the Spirit), the right environment (a clean heart and open mind)** must be present for the seedling of Christ (a new believer) to mature and properly grow.

When Christ redeems us and we are born-again, the seed of righteousness is planted in our heart. Though, this seed of righteousness (or new spirit) planted within may not have spiritually germinated (matured). Yet, this righteous seed causes an individual to become different over time. The heart has been made ready to receive hope, faith, and love undiscovered by the new believer and often those around them. "Therefore if any man be in Christ, he is a new creature: old things are passed away; behold, all things are become new," (2 Cor. 5:17).

To the human mind, it is difficult to conceptualize how God allows or causes a tiny seed to be cultivated, grow, and ultimately produce life. In the Spirit, this same seed of righteousness causes a life-change on the inside. Old patterns of thinking are broken, and a new belief pattern emerges to the surface. As it is written, "John answered and said, a man can receive nothing, except it be given him from Heaven," (Jn. 3:27).

The Holy Spirit is a gift, given to those who obey Him (Acts 5:32). It is a seed of charity planted in our hearts. It is written, "Every good gift and every perfect gift is from above, and cometh down from the Father of lights, with whom is no variableness, neither shadow of turning," (Jas. 1:17).

The seed of love contains the essence of God Himself. We are His offspring. When confessing salvation and being born-again, we should have evidence of Christ living on the inside (or fruit), of a specific nature in our character, mannerisms, and life. "For in Him we live, and move, and have our being; as certain of your own poets have said, For we are also His offspring," (Acts 17:28).

However, for the embryo or "life" that is contained within the seed to germinate and the spirit of Christ to emerge through, an individual's spiritual needs must be fulfilled. They need those three things: water (the Word), warmth (the Holy Spirit and fruits of the Spirit), and the right environment (a clean heart and open mind).

They need water, which is likened to the Word of God. The Word of God has a quickening power. It wakes us up to the power of God, reminding us of the unlimited potential within us. It strengthens us in times of weakness; lifts us up when we are down; guides us when we are lost; rebukes us when we need correction. The Word of God quenches our thirst, filling and renewing our spirit man. This washing of water by the Word, presents us without spot, or wrinkle, Holy and without blemish to God (Eph. 5:26-27). "The entrance of thy words giveth light; it giveth understanding unto the simple," (Ps. 119:130).

A new believer in Christ also needs warmth, which is likened to the Holy Spirit and the fruits thereof (love, joy, peace, patience, kindness, goodness, faithfulness, gentleness, and self-control). "So then faith cometh by hearing, and hearing by the Word of God," (Rom. 10:17).

Growing in God requires us to operate in the Spirit. Our flesh becomes dead when sin no longer has control over our mortal bodies, but the Spirit within us dictates our actions. "It is the Spirit that quickeneth; the flesh profiteth nothing: the words that I speak unto you, they are Spirit, and they are life," (Jn. 6:63).

Spiritual development is a daily task. The more you read God's Word and understand His principles, the more you take on His traits and character. "But there is a spirit in man: and the inspiration of the Almighty giveth them understanding," (Job 32:8). The spirit within you is revealed in your interaction with others, your speech, and your actions. "Either make the tree good, and his fruit good; or else make the tree corrupt, and his fruit corrupt: for the tree is known by his fruit," (Matt. 12:33).

Looking at the fruits of the Spirit from a practical sense, it can refer not only to Christ-like characteristics and/or personality traits that can be witnessed in those around you, but also in other believers in the community. Experienced believers are there to help strengthen those who come to Christ seeking direction. They serve as an example of what the 'personality' of Christ looks like.

Continuing to grow, those new to the faith need to have the right environment, which is likened to a clean heart and open mind. Unless and until a person opens their heart and mind, albeit guarded, they cannot receive the blessings that rain down from Heaven. This is necessary for spiritual maturity. Your heart is the repository of God. We are not talking about your physical heart, but the inner man, the profound aspect of yourself where the Spirit of God dwells. The spirit of righteousness will not sprout in an unclean heart, because the weeds or works of the flesh will choke the life from that seed (Matt.15:18).

When a person opens their mind, they open themselves to the possibility that things can change, that things can and will get better. If they look beyond their current situation or circumstance to imagine the possibilities, and have enough faith in their heart, even the size of a grain of a mustard seed, that is when the Holy Spirit goes to work. Faith, hope, and charity (love) work together to restore the heart. "Create in me a clean heart, O God; and renew a right spirit within me," (Ps. 51:10).

When a person opens their mind and develops the wherewithal and willingness to look at things from a different perspective, they will begin to see things not from their own understanding, but from a more spiritual place. It is in that place where change happens. "And be not conformed to this world: but be ye transformed by the renewing of your mind, that ye may prove what is that good, and acceptable, and perfect, will of God," (Rom. 12:2). Ultimately, the 'right' environment, thus a clean heart and an open mind are achieved through the Word of God.

So, unless these three things—water (the Word), warmth (Holy Spirit & the fruits of the Spirit), the right environment (a clean heart and open mind) are present, the seedling of Christ cannot break through that outer shell (meaning that person's own will). The spiritual germination process (growth) begins when you surrender to God, confess salvation, and allow Christ into your heart.

Now, let's revisit Romans 4:16 which was outlined at that beginning of this course. "Therefore it is of faith, that it might be by grace, to the end the promise might be sure to all the seed; not to that only which is of the law, but to that also which is of the faith of Abraham; who is the father of us all."

We are the seed of Abraham. While he was a natural man who fought a natural battle, he was a faithful servant, and his life serves as an example of both faith and obedience to God. Abraham was not only considered the father of the faithful, but he was also called a friend of God. It was because of his faithfulness that God promised him that he and his descendants would be a great nation.

The same light and power in Jesus, was also in Abraham, and is also in each of us today. This *seed* is the essence of God Himself and as it is stated in 1 John 4:4, "Ye are of God, little children, and have overcome them: because greater is He that is in you, than he that is in the world." The "them" that is referred to here, are those who spread false information and lies. Those that tell you that you are not capable of overcoming your physical impediments and/or your physical challenges in this life. Those who make you feel like you cannot go on to do greater things by the power of Almighty God who He helps you to overcome (1 Jn. 4:1-3).

Let me expound!

Jesus was born of a virgin woman and came through the same 'vicissitudes of life' as you and I. According to the flesh, He was of the seed of David. He was of the lineage of David, which is of the same lineage as Abraham. However, while Jesus was the seed of David according to natural law, He was declared the "Son of God" according to the Spirit of Holiness. "Concerning His Son Jesus Christ our Lord, which was made of the seed of David according to the flesh; And declared to be the Son of God with power, according to the spirit of Holiness, by the resurrection from the dead," (Rom. 1:3-4).

We all are born through a natural law or process. We are born into varied circumstances and conditions that may or may not be considered favorable in the eyes of the world. Some of us at birth, might have been born into situations that would provide us with more advantages than others, such as stable families, financial security, and an easier part of the world to grow and live in, or even a more loving environment.

Others might have been born into poverty, dysfunctional families, or even in a part of the world that has suffered tremendously from the lack of basic resources, such as clean water. Yet, regardless of where we are, or to which condition we have been born into regarding our physical birth, there is a power greater than any physical circumstance, which lies within us. This power gives us the ability to overcome our physical limitations. Your abilities and potential through God are far beyond your physical or natural capabilities.

Jesus had a higher calling on His life; and while Abraham was considered the "father of the faithful," it was and *is* Jesus who became the "light of the world." Jesus our Savior, was always pre-destined to be the Messiah, announced by an angel to Mary and given gifts by kings at His birth. Yet, He tapped into the awesome power within Him and chose to suffer in the flesh for a greater purpose. "Then saith He unto them, My soul is exceeding sorrowful, even unto death: tarry ye here, and watch with me. And He went a little further, and fell on His face, and prayed, saying, O my Father, if it be possible, let this cup pass from me: nevertheless not as I will, but as thou wilt," (Matt. 26:38-39).

We in the flesh, or our physical person and makeup, represent the natural or physical law. Yet, when we accept the principles that Christ stood for and receive salvation, we get in touch with that light within—the light of love and the righteousness of God. This light allows us to do His will and follow God's instruction. We, then, go through another birth process in the spirit, we are born-again and made new. It is through God's divinity and covering that all things are made possible. "But Jesus [looked at] them, and said unto them, With men this is impossible; but with God all things are possible," (Matt. 19:26). The seed within you is powerful, tap into it and reach for the impossible. "Jesus said unto him, If thou canst believe, all things are possible to him that believeth," (Mrk. 9:23).

Each of us has a higher calling on our life, just as Jesus did. He demonstrated how to overcome the limitations of the natural world and what it takes to achieve the supernatural. You too can do great things, but that seed within must be activated. "Believest thou not that I am in the Father, and the Father in me? the words that I speak unto you I speak not of myself: but the Father that dwelleth in me, He doeth the works. Believe me that I am in the Father, and the Father in me: or else believe me for the very works' sake. Verily, verily, I say unto you, He that believeth on me, the works that I do shall he do also; and greater works than these shall he do; because I go unto my Father," (Jn. 14:10-12).

Continuing on, Jesus says in John 14:13-15, "And whatsoever ye shall ask in my name, that will I do, that the Father may be glorified in the Son. If ye shall ask any thing in my name, I will do it. If ye love me, keep my commandments." When all hope seems lost, call on the name of Jesus. The seed of righteousness is within you and there is power in speaking His name. Call unto Him and He will answer and show you mighty things. "That at the name of Jesus every knee should bow, of things in Heaven, and things in Earth, and things under the Earth; and that every tongue should confess that Jesus Christ is Lord, to the glory of God the Father," (Phil. 2:10-11).

Seek God in all things and turn to the Spirit of God that dwells within. God is love, and through the spirit of charity all things are accomplished. Love bears fruit. "Beloved, let us love one another: for love is of God; and every one that loveth is born of God, and knoweth God. He that loveth not knoweth not God; for God is love," (1 Jn. 4:7-8).

The good news is that it is never too late! While you are yet still breathing, you have another chance to change and grow and bear fruit. It is a common salvation, made available to us all. Regardless of the circumstances surrounding a persons' physical birth (being physically born from the works of the flesh), it is through the spirit that we have another chance to change our reality. It does not matter if you were born of fornication or adultery. It doesn't matter if you were born from parents who were murderers, thieves, or liars. It doesn't matter if your life, up until this point, has been one of idleness and wretchedness. If you truly desire success and goodness in your life, it can be brought forth through Jesus. While we may have physically been born of corruption, we are born again of an incorruptible seed by the Word of God (1 Pet. 1:23).

"But if we hope for that we see not, then do we with patience wait for it. Likewise the Spirit also helpeth our infirmities: for we know not what we should pray for as we ought: but the Spirit itself maketh intercession for us with groanings which cannot be uttered. And he that searcheth the hearts knoweth what is the mind of the Spirit, because he maketh intercession for the saints according to the will of God. And we know that all things work together for good to them that love God, to them who are the called according to His purpose. For whom He did foreknow, He also did predestinate to be conformed to the image of His Son, that He might be the firstborn among many brethren. Moreover whom He did predestinate, them He also called: and whom He called, them He also justified: and whom He justified, them He also glorified," (Rom. 8:25-30).

Jesus, the Christ, is the first fruit of those that slept. "I am the vine, ye are the branches: He that abideth in me, and I in him, the same bringeth forth much fruit: for without me ye can do nothing," (Jn. 15:5). When you awaken to the truth within you, any dream in your heart can manifest. It's the power within that is the key to your success.

WORDS OF EMPOWERMENT

1. You cannot corrupt an incorruptible seed, it abides forever. Every seed has to be born and flourish, otherwise it serves no purpose. However, you have purpose, so the birthing of your life's dream will come from the seed within you. You must bring it forth and bringing it forth starts with the acknowledgment that it is present within you. You have to profess those things which you cannot visualize. You must be confident in the hope within you. When you open your mouth, God will give you wisdom. "But the path of the just is as the shining light, that shineth more and more unto the perfect day," (Prov. 4:18).

2. Continue to dream and live by faith. Do not be ashamed of the hope God has set before you. "For I am not ashamed of the Gospel of Christ: for it is the power of God unto salvation to everyone that believeth; to the Jew first, and also to the Greek. For therein is the righteousness of God revealed from faith to faith: as it is written, the just shall live by faith," (Rom. 1:16-17).

3. The more we proclaim what the Word of God has promised, the more we move from hopelessness to faith. "But what saith it? The Word is nigh thee, even in thy mouth, and in thy heart: that is, the Word of faith, which we preach; That if thou shalt confess with thy mouth the Lord Jesus, and shalt believe in thine heart that God hath raised Him from the dead, thou shalt be saved. For with the heart man believeth unto righteousness; and with the mouth confession is made unto salvation," (Rom. 10:8-10).

4. The words that you speak will bring death or life. Speak words that give life to a new you and a new way of thinking and being. "Death and life are in the power of the tongue: and they that love it shall eat the fruit thereof," (Prov. 18:21).

5. A word not spoken is a word not born. The outward man may get weary, but that inward man becomes stronger and stronger (2 Cor. 4:16-18). Keep speaking faith words and manifest your dreams using your communication. The effectual prayers of the righteous availeth much.

6. Do not be discouraged in what you physically see, instead walk by faith (2 Cor. 5:7). God will make the darkness, light. "For thou wilt light my candle: the LORD my God will enlighten my darkness," (Ps. 18:28). The Word of God is a lamp unto our feet and a light unto our path, He keeps making our path brighter and brighter (Ps. 119:105).

7. For your dream to manifest, it must have light. "But all things that are reproved are made manifest by the light: for whatsoever doth make manifest is light. Wherefore, He saith, Awake thou that sleepest, and arise from the dead, and Christ shall give thee light," (Eph. 5:13-14). Give thanks for your dream and for salvation. It shall be even as it were told to you. "Speaking to yourselves in psalms and hymns and spiritual songs, singing and making melody in your heart to the Lord; giving thanks always for all things unto God and the Father in the name of our Lord Jesus Christ," (Eph. 5:19-20).

8. If you are stumbling or asleep; arise! Sing praises with a thankful heart, always praying and praising God. Let God know how much you love and appreciate Him. "But Christ as a son over His own house; whose house

are we, if we hold fast the confidence and the rejoicing of the hope firm unto the end. Wherefore (as the Holy Ghost saith, Today if ye will hear His voice, harden not your hearts, as in the provocation, in the day of temptation in the wilderness: when your fathers tempted me, proved me, and saw my works forty years. Wherefore I was grieved with that generation, and said, They do always err in their heart; and they have not known my ways. So I sware in my wrath, they shall not enter into my rest.) Take heed, brethren, lest there be in any of you an evil heart of unbelief, in departing from the living God. But exhort one another daily, while it is called today; lest any of you be hardened through the deceitfulness of sin. For we are made partakers of Christ, if we hold the beginning of our confidence stedfast unto the end," (Heb. 3:6-14).

9. Allow God to be in control of your life. "For none of us liveth to himself, and no man dieth to himself. For whether we live, we live unto the Lord; and whether we die, we die unto the Lord: whether we live therefore, or die, we are the Lord's. For to this end Christ both died, and rose, and revived, that He might be Lord both of the dead and living," (Rom. 14:7-9). We must have a strong

confidence in His Word until the end or until we receive our promise. When troubles come, go through. You will reap if you faint not (Gal. 6.9). Rest in the Lord and He shall give you the desires of your heart. In His rest, there is peace. Believe until the end, that the work was laid before the foundation of the world (Heb. 3:6-14).

10. "John answered and said, A man can receive nothing, except it be given him from Heaven," (Jn. 3:27). Christ can supply all our needs according to His riches in glory by Christ Jesus. "Do not err, my beloved brethren. Every good gift and every perfect gift is from above, and cometh down from the Father of lights, with whom is no variableness, neither shadow of turning," (Jas. 1:16-17).

11. Wait on the Lord. What you desire of good shall come to pass. Nurture the seed of your ideas with faith and the Word of God. Speak of your dreams as if they were before your eyes. The Scripture says to call those things which be not as though they were. You are taken and snared by the words of your mouth. Remove the weeds of negativity. Sing forth a grateful praise for all God has and is doing in your life.

COURSE FOUR DAILY AFFIRMATIONS

- I will show others love and be kind because the seed of righteousness lives on the inside of me.
- I will speak and operate in the Fruits of the Spirit daily.
- I am not limited by my race, gender, or family situation that I was born into. As a child of God, I understand my opportunities are vast.
- I will praise God for the supernatural.
- I have a higher calling on my life, however it is my responsibility to activate Christ's seed in me.
- I will declare John 15:5.
- I will speak faith-filled works. When I open my mouth, God gives me wisdom.
- I know God will enlighten my darkness. His Word illuminates all that is good in me.
- I will stay connected to God. My faith is rooted and grounded in Him.
- I operate in the Spirit and not in my flesh.
- I will remain happy and always make decisions of good character, that align with His Word.
- God is love. I will show forth charity and forgiveness in my actions towards others.

- I will proclaim the Word of God to strengthen my inner man.

- I have a new way of thinking and being. All good gifts are given from Heaven. I will speak of my dreams as if they were before my eyes.

- I will rest in God and He will give me the desires of my heart.

Study Scriptures to Strengthen You

1 Corinthians 13:13

Jeremiah 29:11

Acts 14:17

Ephesians 3:20

Habakkuk 2:2-3

2 Peter 1:19

Ecclesiastes 11:1-6

Proverbs 4:18

Romans 1:16-17

Psalm 8:1-9

2 Corinthians 4:6-13,17

Genesis 1:11-12, 28-29

Hebrews 6:7

Matthew 18:20

1 Corinthians 2:14

Course 5

Unchain Your Mind

"And be not conformed to this world: but be ye transformed by the renewing of your mind, that ye may prove what is that good, and acceptable, and perfect, will of God," (Rom. 12:2).

"Let this mind be in you which was also in Christ Jesus," (Phil. 2:5).

There is a saying, "Your attitude determines your altitude." This is so true. Basically, what this adage means is that your mindset and the way you look at situations, has a lot to do with what you can and will accomplish in your life. Many things have happened over the course of history. We can blame others for the conditions we might have come through or faced in life, and sometimes, we might have every right to do so. However, today, regardless of what is happening in the world, the only chains that keep us in bondage are the chains we put on our own brains.

The enemy will attempt to wear you out with disappointment, pity-parties, and fear. The Scripture says that he came to frustrate your purpose (Ezr. 4:5).

Yet, God designed for you to be victorious. There is a unique treasure within, so don't fix your mind on your failures, setbacks, your limitations, or shortcomings. Instead, allow God to use you. He makes possible those things, that to many people, seem impossible. "But Jesus beheld them, and said unto them, with men this is impossible; but with God all things are possible," (Matt. 19:26).

Yes, it is true. The enemy will work diligently to place strongholds in your life. He will seek to dominate you through deception, by making you think something other than what is true. Once he has conquered your mind; it gives him power over every other aspect of your life. This is why the Bible says in

Philippians to take on the mind of Christ. In Course Four, we talked in depth about seeds of righteousness and how charity must be firmly rooted in your heart. In order for that to happen, you have to have an open mind and a clean heart for love to grow. No matter what is happening, God can renew your spirit and create in you a clean heart. So, here in Course Five, I want to invite you to delve deep into your own beliefs and show you how to break free from limited thinking and mental bondage. The guiding principle for sharing in Course Five is: *Unchain your mind.*

I want to give you an example regarding limited thinking. Let me tell you a story about a horse. You might have heard it before, but I want to capture it here for you, to think about it in a spiritual context. Universally, the horse symbolizes freedom without restraint. Riding one, appears to make the rider feel like they can "free themselves from all of their restrictions and bindings." In this example, imagine a full-grown horse tied to a small plastic chair. Now the average size of an adult stallion can be anywhere between 885 to 1375 pounds (lbs.), depending on the breed of horse. The average weight, the same horse, could carry comfortably is approximately 15 to 20% of their body weight. So, an average horse the size and weight above could easily carry 240 pounds (lbs.), including tack and rider. The average draft horse can pull about 8,000 pounds (lbs.) alone. The two horses together can pull three times the weight of what they could pull individually.

Now, visualize this same 885-1375 pound (lb.) horse being tied to a tiny plastic chair, constrained and thinking it cannot move. Now, a standard size plastic chair weighs between five and ten pounds (lbs.) The horse, in actuality, can take two steps and as he moved the chair would lift, frolic in the wind, and follow after him. Yet, the horse never budges. It never moves. He never left the area where he was tied up. Why? He did not run away because in his mind, he was being held captive.

The horse recognized being tied to something as an inability to move, regardless of what that "something" may be. Yet no matter how strong the horse was, and regardless of his ability to run with little effort and drag that plastic chair with him, he remains stagnant. The mare's mind is most likely recalling past experiences of trying to walk when his harness was tied, and being yanked back in place. So, as a result of this horse's past experience, he inadvertently stops trying to move. This horse is mentally in bondage and therefore, he remains in physical captivity although he was very capable of moving freely. How many of us can relate to this example?

There are similar stories regarding the flea in the jar, and the elephant tied to the stake. All three stories deal with similar scenarios of a caged mentality. The flea could easily jump out of the jar. The elephant can easily move if tied to a stake. The horse, the flea, and the elephant's lack of freedom was unknowingly - all in their head. There is this photograph online with an image of a horse tied to a blue chair, describing this real scenario. The caption on the photograph reads: "Sometimes the thing that is holding you back . . . is all in your head." This is a true statement!

This is true with many people. Physically, they can accomplish whatever they set out to do. However, their thinking actually limits them. Many believers are like the horse, the elephant, or the flea in these examples. They have been conditioned to believe that they are powerless. They are free, but they do not understand who they are and their amazing potential; consequently limiting themselves.

There were times when human beings were held captive. During slavery, people were beaten into submission and placed in an environment of fear, to keep them obedient to their slave master. Today, people are enslaved by their fears, their thoughts, their finances, and more. They are in bondage. Yet, not because they are physically bound, but because they are in a state of mental bondage. They have chains on their brains.

There is no way to move forward in your life, and accomplish the impossible without removing your mental chains. You must unchain your mind!

The question at this point to ask is, "How do I unchain my mind?"

First of all, think about how you might be bound. What thoughts do you have that keep you in a state of mental bondage? In what ways do you allow limiting beliefs to keep you held back? What food are you feeding your mind, and what is the impact of what you take in daily? Have you seriously asked yourself, "What is holding me back?"

After doing a self-analysis, take a good-long-hard look in the proverbial mirror and the actual mirror if need be, and decide where you want to be in your life? What is it that you want to accomplish? Then, ask yourself: Who you are going to believe? Once you answer those questions, you have to feed your mind for the occasion. Let me explain.

When a fisherman goes fishing, he has to use the right bait to catch the specific fish he wants to catch. If he is looking to hook a catfish, then he may want to use crawfish. However, if he wants to succeed in catching salmon, he may want to look at using roe eggs. The fisherman's methods differ based on what he is trying to accomplish or the type of fish he wants to catch.

Another example is someone who wants to lose weight. If the result you are looking for is to shed pounds, then you may want to up your protein consumption and lower your carb intake. You may also want to boost your metabolism. There are specific things one can do to boost their metabolism. While I won't go into the vast details and options to boost your metabolism, I will define it to clarify my intent. Metabolism is the "process that occurs within living organisms in order to maintain life." Different methods of weight loss can help you achieve real results.

No matter the situation, being in a state of mental bondage is not living. To dream, but to not have the belief or faith that what you see in your mind is possible, is not living. Being physically capable, but lacking the mental tenacity to accomplish your goal, is not living. Freeing your mind is about living a free and abundant life. The media would have you to believe much craziness and keep you in a constant whirlwind of fear. Fear of diseases, fear of natural disasters, fear of war, fear of airborne chemicals, fear of violence, fear of this and that. . . the list can go on and on. Social media, the fashion or entertainment industry, music, and even television can keep you in a state of flux; making you believe everything you hear and see, if you are not careful. It can consistently put you in a frenzy, making you anxious and concerned, if you are not rooted in Almighty God.

Beloved, let no one rob you of your dreams or your destiny! Jesus said, "The thief cometh not, but for to steal, and to kill, and to destroy: I am come that they might have life, and that they might have it more abundantly," (Jn. 10:10).

My point is, while you may be physically strong enough to move forward, sluggishness of mind keeps many people from having the necessary stamina to keep going when things get tough. Sluggishness comes by way of feeding your mind lies, chasing a dollar, and trying to do things the way the world says it ought to be done. Do not chase success; success will inevitably find you when you put God first in your life. "But seek ye first the Kingdom of God, and His righteousness; and all these things shall be added unto you," (Matt. 6:33).

God never said it would be easy. In your quest to fulfill your dreams, trials will come. There will be storms no matter how small or great. However, to have the endurance needed to push through the hardships, you must have a healthy spiritual diet. The slave could not break away from the plantation without being open to possibility. The stallion could not break away from the chair without releasing limiting fears. The man or woman could not lose weight without implementing the proper method for their lifestyle and body type. Therefore, the best thing to do to gain the mental strength to break free from mental bondage is to feed your mind; digest the Word of God.

It is God who sets the captive free. There are at least twenty-six verses in the Bible that bear witness to it being God, who gives freedom. In Jeremiah it says, "'It shall come about on that day,' declares the LORD of armies, 'that I will break his yoke from off their necks and will tear off their restraints; and strangers will no longer make them their slaves," (*New American Standard Bible*, Jer. 30:8).

Transformation, restoration, and the renewing of your mind as discussed in Romans, happens by meditating on the Word. The Word of God penetrates into every fiber of your being and causes a complete transformation to take place in your life. This transformation allows you to reap the benefits of a fruitful and blessed lifestyle which solely recognizes and relies on God. He delivers! He does not force us to His way. He allows us the freedom to choose, His will and His way. When you submerge yourself in His Word, you are able to tap into supernatural wisdom. Then, His mind becomes available to you. **When God controls your mind, it is free.**

Because this is such an important and powerful principle, I want to really drive it home. With that in mind, I would like to briefly share a biblical story that highlights the importance of being steadfast, obedient, and trusting God's ability to deliver.

The Children of Israel were doing very well in Egypt until the rise of a new king. This new leader, Pharaoh, placed the Children of Israel in bondage and ordered the death of male babies in Egypt. God instructed Moses to go to Pharaoh and tell him to set His people free. Moses was afraid and could not speak without stammering. So, God in response to Moses' fear gave him Aaron, as a helper. Moses was placed in the position to face his fear and help his people. Although, he trusted God, it did not necessarily eliminate that fact that he was afraid to confront Pharaoh. Both Moses and Aaron went to Pharaoh and told Pharaoh to allow the time and space for the Israelites to worship their God. Unjustly, he refused and instead exhausted the Israelites further into submission, by increasing their workload.

No matter what Moses and Aaron said to Pharaoh, and no matter what signs God gave, he would not listen. So basically God told Moses not to worry about it, that He would free the Israelites and for him to get ready because he would lead the Children of Israel out of Egypt. At His Word, God sent devastating plagues on Egypt. He first sent frogs, but Pharaoh's heart hardened. He then sent gnats and flies, after a plague to the livestock, and then He bought boils and soon hail on Egypt. Still, Pharaoh's heart was hardened. Then, God sent locusts and after that three days of darkness. Yet, Pharaoh was stubborn. His heart still hardened and he continued to refuse to set the Children of Israel free. Although with each plague, Pharaoh petitioned for relief, his heart still remained set. He was insolent, proud, and disobedient believing that he was all-powerful and beyond reproach.

Lastly, God decided he would send one more upset and sent a message that all first born would die. He instructed Moses and

Aaron to do Passover. After that night, all of the first born were killed. Finally, in his heartache, Pharaoh released the Israelites to go from Egypt.

The Children of Israel were grateful for their freedom, yet they had been in Egypt for some time and had nowhere else to go. They had to not only trust the leadership of Moses and Aaron, but also believe that God would make a way, although with their physical eyes they did not necessarily see a way. Moses and Aaron continued to trust God. Trusting Him to give provision along the arduous journey and that He would deliver, as He said He would.

However, as they traveled the Children of Israel began to murmur and complain about the journey. Along the way, the they began to lose faith in God. They became disobedient and were not steadfast in believing that they would see the Promised Land that God assured Abraham. They constantly grumbled about almost everything and about both Moses and Aaron too.

The Children of Israel were focused on the past and had forgotten all God had brought them through. When they finally arrived, before entering land of Canaan, they first sent twelve scouts into the land. Ten came back with negative reports because they could not see beyond the physical situation, there seemed to be giants in the land.

Moses and Aaron tried to convince the Children of Israel that all would be well, but the Children of Israel wanted to vote for a captain to lead them back to Egypt. They complained that it would have been better to die in Egypt or in the wilderness from hunger than to die from the swords of the people of Canaan, leaving their wives and children to be left for prey. The Children of Israel did not feel they could overtake the enemies in Canaan, although God said they could. So, they turned back in fear and did not trust God.

Consequently, God allowed them to wander in the wilderness until all the older ones died off. So, they never saw the Promised Land, not because God did not deliver, but because they lost hope, faith, and trust in Him. They wandered around for years, as a result of their disbelief in God's power to keep them. God did not allow Moses to see the Promised Land because Moses did not rise above his anger. On the other hand, Aaron's followed God's instruction, using his staff he struck a rock to provide what the people needed. Instead of letting the Children of Israel know that God is the one who made a way, Moses made the people believe that he provided the water.

From Egypt to the wilderness to the Promised Land, there were many lessons to be learned. Those lessons came by way of plagues, the Passover, the Red Sea, God's presence at Mount Sinai, giving of the Ten Commandments, the building of the tabernacle, the quails and manna. Also, all the trials that the travelers experienced from fear, frustration, and hunger.

This story in Exodus teaches us hope, faith, and trust. It teaches us appreciation, gratitude, and obedience. Moses leading the Children of Israel out of Egypt teaches us that no matter what you are going through and no matter who comes up against you, when God calls you for a divine purpose, He will protect you and see you through the trials to achieve it. Through this parable, we can see the power of God and His incredible ability to lead us (like the Israelites) to our destination. It teaches us that no matter what things look like, God can and will meet us where we are and help to bring change our lives. It teaches us that sometimes things appear to get worse before they actually get better, but that we should remain steadfast and trust the power of God. Trusting in His ability to deliver.

No matter what chaos surrounds you, God can still bless you. He can lift you out of that chaotic situation and change your life. In the story of Exodus, the Children of Israel lost faith, they lost hope, and they lost the trust in God. While they remembered He was their Rock, they still cursed Him with their tongue, complaining about all the trials they encountered along the way. The Bible says in Psalm 78:41-42, "Yea, they turned back and tempted God, and limited the Holy One of Israel. They remembered not His hand, nor the day when He delivered them from the enemy."

Beloved, do not be like the Children of Israel (of that time) and turn back on God. Always remember and think of His goodness. Express gratitude for all that He has done for you. Shout Hallelujah and sing His praises. If He did it before; He will do it again. Think back to all He has done in the past, and never stop believing Him. Whatever you ask or think; He can do. He IS God. Remember how He cared for you when others turned their backs on you. Remember how He made a way when you could not see a way. Even now, bear witness to what He is doing in your life today! God is greater than any giant who seeks to harm you. The enemy comes to magnify situations in your life. The battle is in the mind. Your mindset and your attitude about an obstacle, will determine your failure or success. Dreams do not manifest in fear. You will experience battles as you follow your dreams; but remain steadfast and fearless. Keep believing and stand firm in your faith. Keep trusting in God!

In spite of your situation, God desires to bless you. Open your mind to God and remove the chains. When your mind is truly focused on God, you have the ability to usher in His presence. Do not limit God, according to your own limitations. Expand your way of thinking and set it free through His Word. Call those things which are not, as though they already are. You can achieve your dreams and you can have what you desire if it aligns with God's purpose for your life. As long as you continue to put God first. Feed on His Word. The Word of God will never leave you wanting or empty, and God will never forsake you.

"For the Word of God is quick, and powerful, and sharper than any twoedged sword, piercing even to the dividing asunder of soul and spirit, and of the joints and marrow, and is a discerner of the thoughts and intents of the heart," (Heb. 4:12).

WORDS OF EMPOWERMENT

1. For the blessings of the Lord to flow in your life, you must give God full reign and allow Him to work.

2. Release your mind and get in His mind.

3. You have the power within you to create with your words; by speaking whatever you desire, and it shall come forth. Therefore, speak life. Speak words of affirmation; God can and God will. Have faith in God. "Death and life are in the power of the tongue: and they that love it shall eat the fruit thereof," (Prov. 18:21).

4. Put on Christ. Commit yourself to effectively understand His magnificence. Then, you will be able to utilize the tools He has given you through His Word.

5. Wherever the Word of God lives, it is like a river of living water which will never run dry. Wherever the river flows it will bring forth life. It will bring forth your money, house, businesses, and everything else that you desire.
6. God is so good, that He allows us and/or provides us with His wisdom and intellect to choose what will bring glory to His name. He has given us power to say yea and nay, up or down. He has given us the power to choose our own path.

7. Elevate your mind from the Earthly realm and visit God in the Heavens; where everything you need, you can receive. Your peace, your joy, your health, and your wealth can be loosed by the fire within you. Pray and control your mind.

8. Set your mind on things above. Set your mind on whatsoever things are true, honest, just, pure, lovely, and of good report. If there be any virtue, if there be any

praise… THINK on these things (Phil. 4:8). THINK GOD!

9. Bless the name of Jesus. If you want to get your mind under control, direct your focus on God. Drink of the living water that can set you free. Whatever you are bound by; fill yourself up with the Word of God and release. Receive your blessing.

10. Dream big! Broaden your horizons and receive the wonderful reward that God has in store for you.

11. It is not what you see with your natural eye. “Now faith is the substance of things hoped for, the evidence of things not seen,” (Heb. 11:1).

12. Follow God’s instructions in everything you seek to do. You may be enclosed within the membranes of your own mind but if you follow God, it shall come to pass. The barriers and walls hindering you cannot fall in your life until you learn how to shout, until you learn how to praise God and take away the limits. Take God at His Word and win the battle.

COURSE FIVE DAILY AFFIRMATIONS

- I have the authority to speak my mind, as Christ spoke to the raging sea, commanding it to obey. I can open my mouth and speak to my storm… *"Peace be still."*
- In His presence is a fullness of joy, and I will give God control and trust His will for my life.
- I affirm that the sky is not the limit, it is only the beginning and with God all things are possible.
- I bear witness that there is no end to the goodness of God.
- I understand that all opportunities and blessings come from God.
- I will allow the blessings of the Lord to richly flow in my life.
- I will keep my mind on God, and by doing so, usher in the presence of God in my life and circumstances.
- God lives in my praise.
- For every problem in my life, God has provided a solution. Therefore, I will seek God.
- I will allow nothing to hinder my praise.
- The presence and the blessings of the Lord are flowing in my life.

- God is my provider, no matter which vessel or source is used to present the blessing.

- There is nothing that is too hard for my God.

- I will allow God to work through me.

- I will trust God in all things.

Study Scriptures to Strengthen You

Joshua 6:1-20

Psalm 78:41-42

Philippians 3:14

Exodus 16:2-3

Numbers 13:30-33

Numbers 14:9

Hebrews 11:1

Proverbs 18:21

Course 6

Clarify Your Dream

"For I know the plans I have for you, declares the Lord, plans to prosper you and not to harm you, plans to give you hope and a future," (*New International Version*, Jer. 29:11).

"A man's gift maketh room for him, and bringeth him before great men," (Prov. 18:16).

Everyone has a story to tell. Most people have a longing or burning desire in their heart, something they wish they could do or be. Some stories may be great, and some might be simple or seemingly small. However, there is no dream or yearning that should be ignored or passed over as if it were not important. God has a purpose for each and every one of us. From the beginning, prior to our birth, and even at the moment of conception, God had a plan. He had and *still has* an intent for why you exist and why you are where you are now. He has designed your circle of influence and taken into account every person whose life you would impact. Your purpose was determined, even before you were born into the world.

In Course Six, I would like to encourage you to dig deep into your soul—the deepest part of yourself. Dig deep and pull out that burning desire, but also clarify it, make it intelligible, and free from ambiguity. When something is ambiguous, it is vague, lacks the certainty of meaning or intention. God was very decisive when He created you in the womb of your mother. He knew exactly what He was doing. The principle I would like to highlight in this Course is: *Clarify Your Dream.*

God knew you before you came out of your mother's womb. He knew you when He formed you and knew exactly why He was creating you. He blessed you and anointed you. He said you were entitled to respect, regardless of your parent's situation or condition at the time of your conception. God legitimized you! "Before I formed thee in the belly I knew thee; and before thou camest forth out of the womb I sanctified thee, and I ordained thee a prophet unto the nations," (Jer. 1:5).

Regardless of who doesn't find you acceptable or worthy, and despite those who have a problem with you or feel you serve no purpose. God *has* chosen you for this time and for His purpose. He deposited gifts in you to serve His purpose and as the Bible said, those gifts will make room for you. "According as He hath chosen us in Him before the foundation of the world, that we should be Holy and without blame before Him in love," (Eph. 1:4).

Did you know that God will provide you with what you need to accomplish His purpose? Given that God has devised a plan for your life, and has given you a purpose, trust Him to also guide you along the way. You might not have discovered your life's purpose yet. You may not know what you were born to be or do, but what I would like to do is walk with you down the road, to discuss your heart's desire (dream) and hopefully along the way, you will find the path to your purpose. Your dream (heart's desire) must align with God's purpose for your life. Yet how will you know that if you have not clarified your dream? So, in Course Six, we will focus on your aspirations and yearnings; and later on see how those interests line up with God's purpose for your life.

There are five steps to clarifying your dream. These steps are: **1.)** Be honest about what you want; **2.)** Admit to what you want; **3.)** Be specific and definitive about what you want; **4.)** Make the decision that yes, I really want this. Then finally, **5.)** Commit to going after what you want and desire.

Let's discuss these steps in more detail.

Step 1: Be Honest About What You Really Want

The first step to clarifying your dream is to be honest about what you want. Being honest about what you want is not always as easy as it sounds, because sometimes you can almost be crucified for your lofty dreams. With the judgments in the world, especially among church folk or family, you can be made to feel ashamed for having a dream or desire that may not fit into the box that others have placed you in. In their minds and hearts: It's just not possible for you.

Yet, regardless of others skepticism, you must embrace the truth. Be honest with yourself and with God about what you truly desire in your heart. However, being forthcoming does not mean sharing your dream with all of the people you know before it's time. No, that dream must be protected like a baby in the womb. Everyone around you may not support your dreams including friends, family, and others who may be close to you. Later in this course, we will relate and go into the lesson about Joseph and his unsupportive brothers. The truth is only God knows what you are truly capable of. He is the one who has enabled you. Remember to surround yourself with positive people who support your dream, believe in you, and will encourage you along the way.

Step 2: Admit to What you Really Want

When you admit to the truth of something, you let it in; you allow it into your heart and receive it. You do right by it and are faithful to it. That is a huge commitment; but it's a crucial step in clarifying your dream. When you confess your heart's desires to yourself and to God, you open the way for God to bless you for the acceptance of it before it's manifested in the flesh. To not acknowledge the gift that God has placed within you, can cut off whatever blessing can come from it. Consider the parable of the Nobleman traveling to a far country (known as the Bags of gold story) in the Bible in Matthew 25:14-30.

Step 3: Be Specific and Definitive about What you Want

In Mark, chapter 10 in the Holy Bible, it tells of an incident when Jesus and His disciples were in Jericho surrounded by a crowd of people. There was a blind man named Bartimaeus, the son of Timaeus, sitting on the side of the road begging. When he heard that it was Jesus of Nazareth walking, he cried out, "Jesus, thou son of David, have mercy on me!" The crowd was very displeased and so were the disciples. Yet after several cries out to gain His attention, "Jesus, thou son of David, have mercy on me." Jesus asked him to come forward and asked the man, "What wilt thou that I should do unto thee?" At that point, Bartimaeus told Jesus, "Lord, that I might receive my sight." After the man declared to Jesus what he wanted, Jesus said to him, "Go thy way; thy faith hath made thee whole." Immediately he regained his sight and followed Jesus (Mrk. 10:45-52).

The Bible is clear on the importance of being specific and definitive in prayer. Many ask God for what they want, but they are not clear in what they want. So how do you expect God to give you the desires of your heart, when you have not stated clearly what they are? While God is God all by Himself, conversing with Him and asking of Him is likened to you asking your Earthly father and mother for something. You spell it out! The same is true with God. Be specific, and being specific is more for your sake than for God's sake.

Being specific in your request helps to clarify in your own mind and heart, about what you genuinely want. It helps you to define more clearly what your precise needs are. When you know *what* you need, you have a better direction regarding *where* to gain access to those desires. Being specific is challenging. Yet through becoming more specific and definitive, you become closer to God, strengthening your relationship and connection to Him. Being transparent, allows you to engage and communicate with God; open lines of communication strengthen any relationship. When you are clear about what you want, it helps you to recognize the solutions when they come. Be mindful that clarifying your dream, does not justify your request. God is not a genie in a bottle. His process and solutions often take time. God's solution often comes to fulfill our needs and not always satisfy our wants. Be thankful that He knows best!

Finally, being clear increases your faith because in clarifying your goals, you begin to visualize that necessary steps to make them attainable. Thus, increasing your faith and causing you to believe.

Step 4: Make the Decision that 'Yes', I Really Want This

No matter how honest you are with yourself about what you want, and no matter how specific and decisive you are, until and unless you 'say yes' to yourself, there will be no movement toward your dreams. Developing the courage to say yes to your goals, means in contrast that you must say no to anything that will hinder your ability to accomplish them. For some, that can be very daunting. However, this is an obstacle you will have to overcome if you plan on accomplishing your dreams. As the Bible says, you cannot serve two masters. "No man can serve two masters: for either he will hate the one, and love the other; or else he will hold to the one, and despise the other. Ye cannot serve God and mammon," (Matt. 6:24).

Saying 'yes' to yourself is paramount and one of the most important things you can do.

Step 5: Commit To Going After What You Want

So now, you are honest about what you really want; you have admitted to the truth about what you want, you are decisive about what you want, and you have decided to say ***yes***. Now it is a matter of going after it with full commitment. If you take one step toward God, He will take ten steps toward you. When I say commit to going after what you want, I don't mean to "chase" your dream. Going after what you want is about preparing yourself and taking the little daily steps and actions that bring you closer to what is already yours. Don't *chase* anything and do not be anxious. Take small and consistent action steps toward a goal and hold the vision in your mind. Ultimately, through persistence and perseverance, you will achieve it. Having faith is one thing, but putting action behind your faith is another.

"What does it profit, my brethren, if someone says he has faith but does not have works? Can faith save him? If a brother or sister is naked and destitute of daily food, and one of you says to them, 'Depart in peace, be warmed and filled,' but you do not give them the things which are needed for the body, what does it profit? Thus also faith by itself, if it does not have works, is dead," (*New King James Version*, Jas. 2:14-17).

Clarifying your dream, is about lining up action with your words, as to make them congruent. Don't say one thing, but then act opposite of what you say. If you say you want to be a singer, then what are you doing each day to show in your actions that you want to be a singer? To be a doctor, what steps are you taking today for your aspiration to become a doctor to manifest? What actions are you taking now? **The commitment is in the doing!**

In my own life, I have had many ups and downs. Lord knows I have struggled tremendously in my own journey, whether it was with my music, with my family, or attacks from satan against our ministry. It has not been easy. Yet, for me, during every one of the struggles, God continued to bring me to the remembrance of Joseph and the story of his life as outlined in the Holy Bible. As I reflected on the trials that Joseph faced, how God was right there with him, and how he persevered, I became stronger in my spirit to press forward in the midst of all of my own personal storms. I saw myself in the text, as if my story were parallel with Joseph's story. He was an example of perseverance for me as I was facing my own circumstances. I needed that lesson and illustration to help me to see more clearly.

Even though Joseph was repeatedly challenged prior to his dream being made manifest, he ultimately overcame every obstacle he faced. He remained faithful to God and eventually God was glorified in Joseph's situation. Thankfully, he prevailed in spite of all of his opposition. He was a misfit; different than his brothers and distinct from other members of his family. For his siblings, that was difficult to accept. How can a young man, from the same parents, be so recognizably separate from the rest of his family? Joseph's heart was turned towards God and he not only found favor with his Heavenly father, but also his Earthly father, Jacob. I can relate because in my own life, I can recall people saying to my mother, "This little girl of yours doesn't act like the rest of them. There is something different about her."

Jacob had at least thirteen children—twelve sons and one daughter. Joseph was Jacob's youngest son when he was sold into slavery by his brothers, and the only child of his mother Rachel, who had yet to give birth to his younger brother Benjamin. After many years of not conceiving and dealing with bouts of depression because of it, God heard Rachel's cries and blessed her with not only one son, but ultimately another. When Rachel's eldest child, Joseph was born, Jacob was old in age. Because of his age, and because his wife had been barren up to that point in time, Jacob favored his son Joseph above his other sons. He made Joseph a "coat of many colors" demonstrating his love for his youngest son and a representation of God's favor on his son's life. For this reason, Joseph's brothers were envious of him. They hated him and were very unkind to their youngest brother.

One thing that made Joseph "special" was not only did he have prophetic dreams, but he was also gifted with the ability to interpret dreams. When Joseph was a teenager, he had a prophetic dream. In this vision, Joseph saw his brothers bowing down to him. Joseph, being young and immature, shared his dream with his brothers, not realizing that they resented him. They were bitter, having a deep seated envy for him and did not have his best interest at heart. After hearing about the vision, Joseph's brothers became enraged and their hatred for their brother grew. Joseph then had another dream where the sun, the moon, and eleven stars bowed to him. He also shared this dream with his brothers and also his father, unaware of the consequences he would face.

Joseph thought that his family would be excited about his dreams, but they were not. "And he told it to his father, and to his brethren: and his father rebuked him, and said unto him, what is this dream that thou hast dreamed? Shall I and thy mother and thy brethren indeed come to bow down ourselves to thee to the Earth?" (Gen. 37:10).

While his father was noticeably agitated, he continued to reflect on what Joseph shared, but it was another story for the brothers. Some of Joseph's brothers plotted to kill him and throw him in a pit. Then, lie and tell their father that a wild animal had killed him. The eldest brother, Reuben, overheard his brothers' plan for their younger brother and advised them not to kill him, but just throw him in a dry well. Reuben had planned on rescuing him later from the place his siblings had discarded him.

So, the brothers stripped Joseph of his "coat of many colors" and threw him in the pit. As the brothers sat down to eat, they saw a caravan heading to Egypt containing spices. Another brother, Judah, spoke up and said, "Hey, let's not harm him; after all, he is our brother. Let's just sell him to the Ishmaelites (descendants of Ishmael, the elder son of Abraham). So, the brothers all agreed to sell Joseph into slavery. When the Midianite merchants came by, they pulled Joseph out of the pit and sold him to the Midianite slave traders for twenty pieces of silver and Joseph was taken to Egypt. Just for clarity, the Ishmaelites and Midianites are all descendants of Abraham through two of his sons. They are like a nation within a nation and "can be described as the same people with the same father – Abraham."

After being transported to Egypt by these merchants, Potiphar (one of Pharaoh's officials and the manager of his household) bought Joseph from the Midianites. Potiphar recognized that Joseph was peculiar, and therefore he favored him, placing him over all his personal affairs. While Joseph was working for Potiphar, his master's wife tried to seduce him by throwing herself onto him. Yet, Joseph did not allow himself to be tempted by her beauty or her charm. In his integrity, he refused all the advances by Potiphar's wife. She soon became disgruntled and angry at being refused by Joseph. As an act of revenge, she ripped his clothing and consequently Joseph fled from her. However, a piece of his clothing remained with her. At that point Potiphar's wife summoned the guards and accused Joseph of forcing himself upon her. When Potiphar heard the accusation, he became enraged and had Joseph thrown into prison.

Joseph experienced many years of adversity. Yet while he was in prison, he interpreted the dreams of two of Pharaoh's officers—the cupbearer and the baker. It came to pass what Joseph had interpreted. Although Joseph asked the cupbearer to remember him and to mention to Pharaoh what he had done, the cupbearer forgot about Joseph for a time. It was not until Pharaoh's dream greatly troubled him, and he sent out into the city for all the chief magicians, but there were none who could interpret his dreams. It was then the cupbearer spoke up about the Hebrew man who interpreted his dream. So, Pharaoh sent for Joseph to make sense of his vision.

Joseph told Pharaoh there would be seven years of plenty followed by seven years of famine in Egypt. He further instructed Pharaoh according to the knowledge that God gave him through his gift on what to do, and Pharaoh prepared Egypt according to the words of the prisoner Joseph.

Amazingly, what Joseph prophesied came to pass. As a result he found favor with Pharaoh, who then placed him over all of Egypt. Joseph became his second in command, answering to no one but Pharaoh. When the famine came about, in desperation, Joseph's father sent ten of his sons to Egypt to buy grain for bread. Jacob did not send Benjamin, the youngest of the sons. Jacob did not want harm to come to Benjamin.

When Joseph's brothers arrived in Egypt to buy grain, they came and bowed down before the governor over the land of Egypt. Unwitting that it was the brother they discarded and sold years before. Joseph, was assigned the task of selling grain to the land during the famine. His brothers did not recognize him, yet Joseph immediately knew who they were but withheld his identity and treated them like strangers. He spoke roughly to his brothers and accused them of being spies. The brothers were detained for three days and then Joseph, fearing God, retained one and instructed them to go back and take food to their households, but to bring the youngest son to him to verify that they were truthful. Joseph replaced the money in their sacks, plus gave them provision for the journey. He kept and bound him before their eyes.

The brothers remembered what they did to their younger brother. Joseph overheard them discussing what they had done, them not realizing that he was in their midst. Joseph stepped away and wept, then returned to them and sent them away to retrieve their youngest brother. When the brothers returned to their father and realized that all of their monies were returned into their sacks, they became afraid. They told their father what had happened and explained to them that the Lord over Egypt instructed them to bring their younger brother. Their father was upset and said to them, "…You have bereaved me of my children: Joseph is no more, and Simeon is no more, and now you would take Benjamin. All this has come against me," (*English Standard Version*, Gen. 42:36).

Reuben pleaded with his father and said to him that he will return Benjamin and if he didn't, to kill his two sons if he did not keep his word. Jacob refused to allow them to take Benjamin. He said to them, "…My son shall not go down with you, for his brother is dead, and he is the only one left. If harm should happen to him on the journey that you are to make, you would bring down my gray hairs with sorrow to Sheol," (*English Standard Version*, Gen. 42:38).

When the family ran out of food, the father sent them back to Egypt to buy more food. After much discussion and bereavement, Jacob sent his son Benjamin with the brothers along with double the money and gifts for the master over the land. The first to cover the first set of grains, and the second to cover the grain they were to buy. When they arrived with their brother Benjamin, they were invited to have sup with Joseph in his house. The men were afraid, but Joseph calmed their fears. Yet, he was so overcome with emotion he had to hide himself away to cry as he inquired about their father. Joseph gave them food from his table and gave Benjamin five times the amount that the others were given. His brothers, still not knowing who he was, bowed before him and were in dismay.

When it was time for Joseph's brothers to leave, Joseph had the caravan set up by putting silver back in the mouth of his brothers' sacks, and a silver cup in Benjamin's sack. He then instructed his men to go after them as if they had stolen the cup and instructed the one with the cup shall be seized. When they returned to Joseph's house, and Joseph accused them of stealing, they begged Joseph not to keep Benjamin, as it would kill their father.

After listening to his brothers' pleading to spare his father, Joseph could not help but to reveal himself to his siblings as he was overcome with emotion, so much so that the entire house heard, Pharaoh's house heard. After hearing that Joseph's brothers were in Egypt, Pharaoh released wagons, donkeys, provisions, and more and told them to bring their father, wives, and families to Egypt and they will be provided with the best of the land of Egypt.

When they returned to their father in the Land of Canaan, their father did not believe them when they said that Joseph was still alive. It was not until he saw the wagons, the silver, the donkeys, and provision that he believed them. So Joseph's entire family returned to Egypt, as to survive the next five years of famine in the land.

"So Israel took his journey with all that he had and came to Beersheba, and offered sacrifices to the God of his father Isaac. And God spoke to Israel in visions of the night and said, 'Jacob, Jacob.' And he said, 'Here I am.' Then he said, 'I am God, the God of your father. Do not be afraid to go down to Egypt, for there I will make you into a great nation. I myself will go down with you to Egypt, and I will also bring you up again, and Joseph's hand shall close your eyes," (*English Standard Version*, Gen. 46:1-4).

This story is lengthy and detailed but relevant. God has a plan for your life, just as he had a plan for Joseph's life. Like Joseph, you might experience adversity, but as you continue to use your gift, as the Bible says in Proverbs 18:16, your gift will open doors for you.

Joseph's story teaches us to be mindful of whom we share our desires and dreams with. "Give not that which is Holy unto the dogs, neither cast ye your pearls before swine, lest they trample them under their feet, and turn again and rend you," (Matt. 7:6). I learned this lesson the hard way too. I learned that everybody will not share your enthusiasm. Sometimes when you share information with others, those who are jealous or envious of you will intentionally try to hinder you from accomplishing your goals. As I kept being taken back to the story of Joseph, God did not allow me to have rest until I internalized it and learned valuable lessons from his story and life. I was blessed to recognize that Joseph never lost sight of his dreams.

Sometimes people look at your situation from the outside and perceive a reality, that in truth does not exist. They look at what you have, but do not realize what suffering and setbacks came along with obtaining it. They don't readily understand the trials you have had to face or the struggles that you went through, to obtain what you possess or achieve where you are in your life. Being in ministry has taught me many valuable lessons.

The enemy has plotted to destroy my family through lies, scandals, negative media coverage, and social media. He has even attempted to use family, friends, and others against us. Yet, God gave us power to press forward; for He was and is with us.

Sometimes, the 'fire' of a life situation and trial can be intense. Yet it is purposeful. During the fire, in the middle of the scorching heat, you must remain focused on God. Maintain a steadfast mind to be victorious. When you believe and trust in God and His Word, nothing can defeat or discourage you! Know that you are more than a conqueror and that the battle is already won. You have to know that the battle is not even yours, it belongs to God. So, why sit around disquieted about what others may say or do against you? You know the truth; therefore, move and operate in the knowledge of that truth! Don't give up on your dreams because of the adversity. If you persevere in the fire; your dreams surely shall come to pass.

"They shall lift up their voice, they shall sing for the majesty of the Lord, they shall cry aloud from the sea. Wherefore glorify ye the Lord in the fires, even the name of the Lord God of Israel in the isles of the sea," (Isa. 24:14-15).

Anyone seeking greatness and living their life according to the calling of God, will face obstacles. Sometimes those challenges are big and sometimes they are exceedingly small. I can recall the various trials I went through and still go through in my life. Sometimes they can be enough to make you feel ashamed because of the way others look down on you or question your moral integrity. When people do not understand the plan of God on your life, they will see your trials as something you should be ashamed of; but I'm here to tell you that you should never be ashamed. Those events were only tests that ultimately become a part of your testimony! "...tribulation worketh patience; and patience, experience; and experience, hope: and hope maketh not ashamed; because the love of God is shed abroad in our hearts by the Holy Ghost which is given unto us," (Rom. 5:3-5).

God allows trials to take place to help purify us. As I reflect back again on the story of Joseph, what he went through was all a part of God's plan. Even though Joseph went through a lot, God was always right there with him, working it out for him, and helping him to grow. Joseph never lost hope. He continued to give God the glory. This is why it is important to allow God to complete His plan in and through you, and you will see His hand in every experience. God turns what the enemy meant for bad, and as a tool to hurt you, into a situation which ultimately works out good for you in the end. "But as for you, ye thought evil against me; but God meant it unto good, to bring to pass, as it is this day, to save much people alive," (Gen. 50:20).

Joseph's life is a true testimony of persevering in the midst of trouble. Likewise, it is an example of being clear and allowing your words to line up with your actions. Joseph knew what he wanted, and he let nothing deter him from that. He relied on God in all of his misfortunes. In the end, Joseph led his family, reconciled with his brothers, and saved his people. He waited patiently on the Lord and it was worth the wait. He never doubted God. Genesis 37 describes the story of Joseph in great detail. Believe me when I say, it is worth a read and study! There are also good movies out there about his life. Again, worth the watch!

In this Course, I will leave you with the following. There are three valuable lessons to learn from Joseph that will help you realize your dreams:

1. Never give up in the midst of adversity.
2. Keep your focus on your God and your goal, especially when the enemy sends a distraction.
3. Stay connected to God even when your dreams become a reality.

WORDS OF EMPOWERMENT

1. When you find yourself in a pit, mistreated, and misunderstood; do not rise up in anger, instead trust God and allow the circumstances to elevate you to higher heights in Him. Do not lose your focus in the pit.

2. Look at your trials as something to help purify you and to develop your character.

3. Remember that God never forsakes us, or leaves us comfortless in a trial; and His Word never fails.

4. Continue to press forward in Jesus and know that if you have the faith the size of the grain of a mustard seed, you can move the mountains in your life.

5. As you move forward in your dreams, be mindful of distractions. Be careful not to set up other gods (or idols), besides Almighty God.

6. Put on your full armor of God and stay prepared for battle. When equipped for battle in your mind and heart, nothing shall by any means hurt you.

7. Gird up your loins with truth, as to not allow the enemy to carry you downward to a place in your mind that can only hinder your dreams.

8. Always see the horizon above the clouds. It's in the valley that you will develop a grateful praise, humility, perseverance, faithfulness, and commitment.

9. Although your dreams might be challenged and you may be presented with obstacles, continue to trust God to bring you through. Blessings will be waiting for you to receive once you have come through the trials.

10. God has a plan for your life, continue to seek His guidance along the way and continue to prepare for your time to stand fully in your calling.

11. Always remain grounded in God so you may become a blessing to others.

12. God is Alpha and Omega, the beginning and the end. He knows the outcome of your dreams from the very beginning. It is up to you to remain faithful, steadfast, and patient. So, do not give up! God's Word will not fail.

13. Keep your eyes on the Lord and align yourself with His righteousness. He will open doors for you and your gifts will make room for you. Be refreshed in your spirit and as the Bible says, "Follow peace with all men, and Holiness, without which no man shall see the Lord," (Heb. 12:14).

14. Have faith in God and in your ability to manifest your dreams. Nevertheless, remember that faith without works is dead. Therefore, take daily action steps to usher in the fulfillment of your dreams and goals.

COURSE SIX DAILY AFFIRMATIONS

- I will not lose faith in my dreams, for I possess the favor of God.
- I will rely on God daily, as He is the giver of gifts and it is He who lifts me up.
- I affirm to live my life with integrity and to continuously seek God's face.
- I keep my faith and trust in God for the battle belongs to Him and in Him I am victorious.
- With God all things are possible.
- I bear witness that God is able.
- I am blessed.
- I believe in my dreams and can achieve everything that God has placed on my heart.
- The Lord can bless me with everything needed to fulfill my purpose.
- The power of God worketh through me.
- Through every moment, God is preparing me for my work and service to His people.

Study Scriptures to Strengthen You

Ephesians 1:4-23

Matthew 25:14-30

Genesis 37

Isaiah 45:7

1 Thessalonians 5:18

1 Peter 2:9

Acts 7:9

Daniel 7:25

James 1:6-8

Hebrews 12:14

Course 7

Align Your Dreams with God's Purpose

"And we know that all things work together for good to them that love God, to them who are the called according to His purpose," (Rom. 8:28).

"In whom also we have obtained an inheritance, being predestinated according to the purpose of Him who worketh all things after the counsel of His own will," (Eph. 1:11).

When God gives you a dream or vision for your life, He covers you with His favor so that ultimately your dream can become realized. This favor upon your life is unique and attached to the fulfillment of what you were born to do. A person's dream or vision is specifically tailored to the purpose and will of God. Interestingly, many people have aspirations, yet they don't know the purpose for which they were born. Therefore, they often run around in circles when trying to establish their goals. Aligning your dreams with God's purpose for your life is about discovering His intention. Then, discerning how your ambitions are connected to that purpose. Your dream and life's purpose coincide.

In Course Seven, I would like to discuss how to: *Align Your Dreams with God's Purpose.*

To align something is to bring it into position with, to coordinate, or match it with something else. In this context, what I'm saying is to coordinate your dreams with God's purpose for your life. Let me explain using Joseph and his coat of many colors again, as an example.

Joseph wore a coat of many colors, which was given to him by his father Jacob. His father recognized him to be the future prophet of God, following the destined lineage from Abraham. The coat was a reminder of his royal priesthood and a symbol of his purpose. Jacob had foresight, and was keenly aware that he and his son, Joseph, had a higher calling on their lives. The coat told a story and everything about it was significant. God placed the story of Joseph on my heart and brought to the forefront of my mind, the coat. I realized that the coat differentiated him from his brothers. It represented God's favor in Joseph's life and the life of those who descended from him. As I continued to study his story and look deeper into the coat that Jacob gave his son, I was encouraged spiritually about the unfolding of my own dreams. I understood a deeper significance behind the coat. The multi-colored coat given to Joseph represented the many nations and its inhabitants. It represented the covenant that God made between Him and His people, of Heaven and Earth.

"I have set my rainbow in the clouds, and it will be the sign of the covenant between me and the Earth," (*New International Version*, Gen. 9:13).

Joseph was given the coat in the midst of the conflict with his brothers. They were envious of him and because of that envy, they sought to kill him. Yet, the coat was a sign of God's favor that would inevitably come upon Joseph even in gloom, hardship, and great struggle. The coat was a sign and reminder of God's covenant and promise. This is what is meant by, "God setting his rainbow in the clouds." The colors of the rainbow are: red, orange, yellow, green, blue, indigo, and violet. I knew the colors were important, and God placed on my heart the meaning of most of the colors.

Later on, as I continued to study, a deeper significance of the colors on his apparel came to the forefront. Although the colors may mean something else to you, for me and what God was doing in my life, the colors symbolically represented the items shown below:

Red – The red in Joseph's coat is symbolic of the blood of Christ and His afflictions. Although He was innocent, His love for mankind compelled Him to accept His suffering. Jesus endured the hardship and the struggles, but never lost sight of His purpose. Now, He sits at the right hand of the Father. His life was and is not in vain (Isa. 53:3-12).

Looking at the color red from another perspective, it is symbolic of fire, blood, and the carnal world. It is associated with energy, war, danger, strength, and power. It represents action, confidence, courage, vitality, love, and forgiveness. Also, cleansing, justification, sin, the wrath of God, judgment, and the Cross.

Orange – The color orange within Joseph's coat represents vitality with endurance, power, healing, joy, and creativity. It is symbolic of determination, praise, warfare, passion, fire, and fruitfulness. The color orange reminds us to rejoice and to be vibrant, making a feast to celebrate all the good things that God is doing in our lives.

The lesson of orange is to pick yourself up and shout with a voice of triumph. Work together and not against one another; for God is doing great things and He wants to help you fulfill your purpose.

Yellow – The yellow is symbolic of great communication and carries the promise of a positive future. It represents joy, happiness, wisdom, intellect, energy, purity, and hope. It is a sign of God's glory, Holiness, and purification.

Joseph's coat was taken from him, but they could not take away His character. He was obedient to God, and God was with Him in everything that He experienced. Joseph glorified God in all of his ways, therefore his path was directed by God (Prov. 3:5-6). By being faithful towards God, God was faithful toward him. He acknowledged it was God working in him and not his own abilities.

Green – The color green in Joseph's coat is symbolic to self-respect, well-being, balance, learning, growth, and harmony. It also represents endurance, mercy, and God's Holy seed. Looking at it from another perspective, it represents sowing and reaping, life, nature, fertility, renewal, and rebirth.

God has given us everything we need to survive this Earthly world. He has given us the wisdom of when to plant and governs the appropriate time to reap. He teaches us the law of reciprocity; you will harvest whatever you sow. "While the Earth remaineth, seedtime and harvest, and cold and heat, and summer and winter, and day and night shall not cease," (Gen. 8:22).

Blue – The blue in Joseph's coat symbolizes youth, spirituality, truth, peace, and trust. Also, it represents loyalty, wisdom, confidence, faith, and intelligence. Looking at blue from another perspective, it also represents prayer, priesthood, authority, grace, divinity, the Holy Spirit, being an overcomer, and the Word of God.

Blue encourages us to wait on God to move on our behalf. It reminds us to continuously watch and pray because a strong prayer life will strengthen your faith.

Indigo – The color indigo is symbolic of our intuition and ability to perceive from a spiritual reality. Indigo in Joseph's coat teaches us to keep our minds on God and the dreams He has placed in our hearts and minds. It is a reminder that the battles we face are not carnal, but rather spiritual. And our fight is not in the flesh but in high places. "For we wrestle not against flesh and blood, but against principalities, against powers, against the rulers of the darkness of this world, against spiritual wickedness in high places," (Eph. 6:12).

Indigo represents integrity, dignity, and sincerity. It also represents the ability to look beyond ordinary circumstances to see the magnificence of God's love and His power moving in our lives. Indigo inspires us to look deeper into our experiences so that we may discover our life's purpose.

Violet – Joseph's coat was also adorned with violet. This color is symbolic of wisdom, spirituality, the future, and the imagination. Violet, sometimes called purple, is the color of people seeking spiritual fulfillment. It conveys wealth and it symbolizes royalty, good judgment, and ambition.

Despite Joseph's many trials along the way, he became prosperous and he also helped Egypt prosper, by following the guidance of the Lord. When people of that time praised him, he always turned them right back to God. He acknowledged God as the source of the blessings and the prosperity upon the land. He consistently taught the people to remember that God is the giver of gifts, the source of all wealth and prosperity.

The above colors are seven colors of the rainbow. The coat that Joseph wore, as stated above, was symbolic as each color was also symbolic. The rainbow mentioned in the scripture is also important. A rainbow happens when the sun and rain combine. Sunlight is comprised various colors; however, we do not readily see those colors. When the light of the sun comes to the Earth, the light itself is white. Yet, when the light of the sun touches the rain, depending on the direction or angle that it hits, the water will reflect the color you see. As the light of the sun hits the rain, it separates into the colors we see, causing a rainbow. Yet, the light source is one color initially and only appears to be many different hues by the projection of light energy.

When you study the symbolism of the sun and the symbolism of the rain, it is amazing what may be revealed. I embraced the revelation that God showed me in studying each color that appeared in Joseph's coat. I applied these lessons in my life and gained a better understanding of my purpose and realized how my experiences, dreams, and purpose were parallel.

Everything God has placed in my hands to do; the credit and the glory all belongs to Him. I live, move, and devote my entire being to my purpose because of the God in me. His purpose for my life is ultimately my purpose and my dream. What God wills for me to do, I live and love to do. I understand that the Children of God function at a higher level of greatness when they stay in alignment with God and when they know who they are in Christ. When you align your dreams with God's purpose, it is difficult to get thrown off course.

WORDS OF EMPOWERMENT

1. Live to embody the Holiness of God. Allow His light to shine through you, and as a result prayerfully you will draw others to Him.

2. Do not allow yourself to be distracted from the things God has ordained for your life.

3. Just as God used the colors in Joseph's coat as a representation to motivate and nurture the plan He had for Joseph's life, let that to motivate you for the plans that God has for your life.

4. Exercise your faith to develop excellence, intelligence, self-control, steadfastness, piety, brotherly affection, and Godly love.

5. When pursuing your dreams, do not allow your mind to become infiltrated with anything that hinders righteous thoughts.

6. If there is any goodness and excellence in a situation, if it is worthy of praise: fix your mind on these things. Do those things which ye have learned, received, heard, and seen. God will make everything work together for His aspiration is in your heart. "Finally, brethren, whatsoever things are true, whatsoever things are honest, whatsoever things are just, whatsoever things are pure, whatsoever things are lovely, whatsoever things are of good report; if there be any virtue, and if there be any praise, think on these things. Those things, which ye have both learned, and received, and heard, and seen in me, do: and the God of peace shall be with you," (Phil. 4:8-9).

7. Let the Word of God give you confidence and prepare you to withstand each attack that comes, which is designed to weaken your capacity to fulfill God's purpose in your life.

8. Let salvation, righteousness, peace, faith, and the Truth work for you; for they are more than words. Learn to apply them into your daily walk as God orchestrates the manifestation of your dreams.

9. Enter into the place God prepared for you. In this dwelling you have access to everything you need in Him.

10. Seek to help one another and exercise your NOW faith. Your faith is a powerful gift. God has given us the ability to call those things which be not as though they were.

11. Without faith it is impossible to please God. When you approach God, first and foremost, believe that He exists and that He is able to answer all who diligently seek Him (Heb. 11:1, 6).

12. When you face trials, remember to walk like you are victorious.

13. God's Word is greater than a surgeon's scalpel and can reach into the spirit of man to cut away doubt and fears. We have an open door to our High Priest and it is up to each individual person to take advantage of the accessibility to Christ.

14. You are more than a conqueror. There is nothing of good that God will withhold from you when you walk

upright and trust in Him. He knows what is in your heart.

15. Be diligent to exercise that which God has given you. Avoid slothfulness and procrastination.

16. Put your hands on the plow, get to work and don't look back.

17. Praise God and thank Him for everything, stop complaining when you cannot have your way and when others disappoint you. Praise God, for He has a plan for your life. "But as it is written, Eyes hath not seen, nor ear heard, neither have entered into the heart of man, the things which God hath prepared for them that love Him," (1 Cor. 2:9).

18. When you put your faith in God, He reveals His Truth, and your life becomes an example to others. So, keep a firm grip on your faith and press your way to the finish line. Everything you face is a stepping stone to where God is taking you.

19. Stay connected to Almighty God and He will bless you to produce a great harvest.

20. There is power in the name of Jesus and no matter what is going on in your life, you have the power to speak to the situation and command it to be moved. Shift your world through faith. There is nothing too hard for God and when you speak the Word of God, those circumstances have to obey the voice of the Lord. The Word of God will correct everything. It is to your advantage to rejoice in Him who made it all possible. Have faith in God. His Word is true. He will never leave you nor forsake you!

21. Set your hope wholly and unchangeably on God's divine favor over your life, "For thou, Lord, wilt bless the righteous; with favor wilt thou compass him as with a shield," (Ps. 5:12).

22. God has given you favor and so now you have to exercise it and obtain the promise. Do not let your guard down. Continue to stay balanced with a sober mind in your word and prayers. Be vigilant. Stay watchful and on

alert. Fortify your mind with the Word of God and know the battle is already won through Jesus Christ our Lord.

23. Sow into good ground to reap a harvest.

24. Never allow the actions of others to make you harbor anything against them in your heart because it can hinder your blessings.

COURSE SEVEN DAILY AFFIRMATIONS

- My dreams are connected to the assignment that God has given me, and I am reminded to complete it.
- I exercise my faith daily to develop excellence, intelligence, self-control, steadfastness, piety, brotherly affection, and Godly love.
- I shall set my mind to think on what is valid, trustworthy, righteous, authentic, divine, beautiful, and noble.
- God hears my prayers.
- I am fit for God through our Lord Jesus Christ.
- Everything I have ever hoped for is right in front of me.
- My faith is a powerful gift.
- I powerfully speak my hopes and dreams into existence.

- God has chosen me above all others to do what I was born to do.
- I am as bold as a lion; therefore, I set the time for my dreams.
- I operate in the fullness of my rights; and I am unstoppable through Christ Jesus!
- Nothing is impossible for God. He is ready to give me whatever I need.
- I will stay my course with committed faith and receive the promise.
- My dreams are possible!
- The fire of God that dwells within me cannot be put out.
- God is the true vine and every branch abiding in Him must produce fruit.
- I will lean confidently on Christ; for He is my peace.

Study Scriptures to Strengthen You

Colossians 1:21

Isaiah 53:3-12

Philippians 4:8-9

Ephesians 6:10-17

Romans 4:17-25

Proverbs 3:5-6

Romans 5:1-2

Ephesians 6:18

1 Peter 2:9

Ephesians 3:1-21

Luke 10:19

Hebrews 4:13-16

St. John 9:4

1 Peter 2:20-25

Nehemiah 8:10

Philippians 4:4

Psalm 67:5-6

1 Timothy 1:18

Hebrews 1:7

John 15:1-2, 5, 7

Mark 11:22-24

Isaiah 26:3

1 Peter 1:13

1 Peter 5:8

Deuteronomy 8:18

Study Scriptures to Strengthen You

Hebrews 6:11-15

Genesis 9:3

Matthew 6:12-13

Galatians 6:7-8

Ephesians 2:14

Course 8

Remove Doubt and Develop the Faith to Float

"If any of you lack wisdom, let him ask of God, that giveth to all men liberally, and upbraideth not; and it shall be given him. But let him ask in faith, nothing wavering. For he that wavereth is like a wave of the sea driven with the wind and tossed," (Jas. 1:5-6).

"For verily I say unto you, That whosoever shall say unto this mountain, Be thou removed, and be thou cast into the sea; and shall not doubt in his heart, but shall believe that those things which he saith shall come to pass; he shall have whatsoever he saith," (Mrk. 11:23).

The guiding principle for Course Eight is: *Remove doubt and develop the faith to float.* This is an important principle because faith is the activator for what you want to achieve. It is the very thing that sets in motion the 'thing' you desire. Having faith is acceptance and agreement with the truth of a statement, although there is incomplete evidence. It remains to be physically seen.

There is a saying that goes, **"Let your faith roar so loud that you can't hear what doubt is saying!"** While it is natural to have doubt sometimes, especially if you are looking through your carnal eyes, one must push through doubt to develop strong faith.

Having a desire or a dream is not enough if one wants to experience their purpose fully. Believe that it exists and only needs to be made manifest in the physical world. It takes faith to make that happen. Not seeing the tangible evidence of a thing, is not proof or an indication that something does not exist. However, seeing a physical manifestation of a dream is evidence of faith that conquered doubt. It shows forth works that demonstrated faith. "Yea, a man may say, Thou hast faith, and I have works: shew me thy faith without thy works, and I will shew thee my faith by my works," (Jas. 2:18).

Many people create "bucket lists." These lists are plans of what they hope to accomplish, prior to the end of their natural lives. Too often, though, years pass by and the list of hopes and dreams remain incomplete. In scripture, the Children of Israel wandering in the wilderness is a classic example of an incomplete desire. They wandered for forty years delaying taking possession of the land that God had promised them. Their vision was clear, but their faith was shaky. They doubted their ability, not fully understanding that it was God who would strengthen them. They had the vision and the desire, but they could not push past their doubt. This is why Jesus says in the Bible, "Jesus said unto him, If thou canst believe, all things are possible to him that believeth," (Mrk. 9:23).

On the contrary, an example which demonstrates pushing past doubt to accomplish a goal, can be seen in the story of the Israelites as told in Hebrews 11:30. The Israelites marched around the wall for seven days, believing God that the walls of Jericho would come down. Despite how surreal it seemed, the Israelites obeyed God and the wall came crashing down after the seventh day. If they had stopped believing, the walls would never have fallen. Some may have been doubtful at some point, yet they remained steadfast and obedient to God. This is a classic example of developing the faith to float. To float is to "rest on the surface of the water." It is to release and allow God to take control. Obedience requires faith. It took faith for the Israelites to believe God and follow His instructions to victory.

See, in the example above the Israelites did not lean on their own strength. It was by faith the walls of Jericho fell down, after they were compassed about seven days.

> *"By faith Isaac blessed Jacob and Esau concerning things to come. By faith Jacob, when he was a dying, blessed both the sons of Joseph; and worshipped, leaning upon the top of his staff. By faith Joseph, when he died, made mention of the departing of the children of Israel; and gave commandment concerning his bones. By faith Moses, when he was born, was hid three months of his parents, because they saw he was a proper child; and they were not afraid of the king's commandment. By faith Moses, when he was come to years, refused to be called the son of Pharaoh's daughter; Choosing rather to suffer affliction with the people of God, than to enjoy the pleasures of sin for a season; Esteeming the reproach of Christ greater riches than the treasures in Egypt: for he had respect unto the recompense of the reward. By faith he forsook Egypt, not fearing the wrath of the king: for he endured, as seeing him who is invisible. Through faith he kept the passover, and the sprinkling of blood, lest he that destroyed the firstborn should touch them. By faith they passed through the Red sea as by dry land: which the Egyptians assaying to do were drowned. By faith the walls of Jericho fell down, after they were compassed about seven days. By faith the harlot Rahab perished not with them that believed not, when she had received the spies with peace. And what shall I more say? for the time would fail me to tell of Gedeon, and of Barak, and of Samson, and of Jephthae; of David also, and Samuel, and of the prophets: Who through faith subdued kingdoms, wrought righteousness, obtained promises, stopped the mouths of lions. Quenched the violence of fire, escaped the edge of the sword, out of weakness were made strong, waxed valiant in fight, turned to flight the armies of the aliens. Women received their dead raised to life again. . ." (Heb. 11:20-35).*

It is by faith coupled with action that your dreams will manifest into a tangible reality! Faith without works is dead. "Even so faith, if it hath not works, is dead, being alone," (Jas. 2:17). "For as the body without the spirit is dead, so faith without works is dead also," (Jas. 2:26).

Faith is a decision. Resting on the surface of the water is about rising above your doubt and fears. Developing the faith to float requires certainty. You cannot be double-minded or fearful when you want God's help. Victory requires a certain mindset. It takes having a "Christ-like Mindset," an approach that is willing to act on what you say you believe. It is possessing the confidence in God to help you to bring that action or desire to pass.

Let's look at the parable in Matthew when Jesus fed the multitude and when He and Peter walked on water.

After hearing about the news of John, Jesus withdrew to a private place for solace. When the people heard about this, from the various towns, they followed Jesus on foot. When Jesus saw the crowd, he was touched and empathetic, so He healed the sick among them. As it got later in the day, the disciples encouraged Jesus to send the crowds away so they could make it back to their villages to eat. Jesus insisted not to send them away and instead told the disciples to feed the people. The disciples complained that it was not enough food as there was only five loaves of bread and two fish. However, Jesus giving thanks to God broke the bread and fed 5,000 men, women, and children and even had twelve baskets full of broken pieces of bread. Everyone ate and everyone was satisfied.

Immediately afterwards, Jesus instructed the disciples to go ahead of Him in the boat and head for the other side. Meanwhile, He dismissed the crowds and then retreated up the mountainside for solitude and prayer. By nightfall, Jesus was alone up the mountain, and the boat was in the middle of the water being pummeled by waves due to the strong winds. Just before sunrise, Jesus miraculously began walking on water. The disciples saw Him strolling on the sea water and became terrified. They thought it was a ghost and fear consumed them. Jesus, seeing they were afraid told them to not be afraid and revealed His identity. He told them to take courage. Peter spoke up and said to Jesus, "…Lord, if it is You, command me to come to You on the water,"(*New King James Version*, Matt. 14:28). So Jesus, told Peter to come.

Without really thinking about it, Peter got out of the boat, and began walking on the water toward Jesus. However, when he saw the powerful wind, he became afraid and consequently started to sink. Peter then cried out for Jesus to save him. At that point, Jesus reached out His hand and grabbed Peter. Once He caught Peter, He said, "...You of little faith," He said, "why did you doubt?" (*New International Version,* Matt. 14:31).

Did you notice how Peter walked on water without thinking about it, until he became afraid and doubt crept in?

Imagine being one of the disciples on that boat. You are in the midst of the sea when suddenly the boat is being tossed to and fro from the raging winds. Imagine looking out in the distance and you see a figure coming toward you, but the person looks as if they are floating on air. It's foggy and you can't make out who or what it is. As He gets closer, you see this entity is walking on the sea. Your natural reaction would be to cry out in fear. Who's there? What are you? Who are you? Is this a spirit? You might even wonder if it was a mirage.

In this parable, Peter joined Jesus on the water and took steps in faith out of the boat. Following Jesus' instruction, he walked on the water toward Him. This was truly a miracle, but for Peter, initially he did not even think about what he was doing, he just did it because His Lord told him to. However, as he walked towards Jesus, a strong wind came and as a result his focus changed, and Peter became afraid. In his panic, he was distracted and started sinking under the water. What would you have done? Would you let fear consume you?

Like Peter, many people lack the faith necessary to float. In this context, floating is the ability to trust God and stand firm on His Word. All too often, individuals go through storms in their lives and instead of standing firm on the Word of God, they become distracted by the wind. The 'winds' are the circumstances in your life that may not be favorable such as a lack of money, health issues, a troubled relationship or marriage, problems with your children, and a host of other things. This whirlwind of trouble that comes can sometimes cause a person to lose faith and then become submerged under the mountains in their life.

Similarly to the story about Peter, in the Book of Mark, we are told of a great storm of wind. The water came gushing inside the boat where the disciples were. Jesus was also in the boat. He too witnessed the waves crashing against the boat and flooding the boat. Nevertheless, Jesus remained calm, but the disciples were in a state of panic.

"Master, carest thou not that we perish?"

With great calm and ease, Jesus arose and rebuked the wind, and said unto the sea, "Peace be still."

In an instance, the wind ceased, and there was a great calm. His words to His disciples were, "Why are ye so fearful? How is that ye have no faith?" They feared exceedingly, whispering to one another, "What manner of man is this, that even the wind and the sea obey him?"

Do you have the faith to float? Even if your faith is not that strong, do you have the wherewithal to trust God and allow Him to lead you and sustain you when you can't stay on top of the waters in your life on your own? Do you have the capacity to submerge yourself in His Word?

I asked myself those questions many days. Since early childhood, my dreams have always seemed bigger than life. I was creative and my thoughts were "outside of the box." The way I perceived things, appeared to differ vastly from others around me.

Funny enough, some people viewed me as being eccentric. However, regardless of what other people thought about my manner of being, I leaned on God for strength and confidence. As young as I was, I still went for it! My mind was always on God. He created the moon and the stars, and He created man from the dust of the earth. I knew the God I served was a miracle worker, a healer, a strong and omnipotent God. He works masterfully in a realm all by Himself. So, I placed my trust and my faith in Him. I believed that I could do anything through Him.

Although I had strong faith, it was not always that way. There was a time when I was haunted by fear. I lived in a state of anxiety. I feared failing; I feared people, and many other things. I was bound by a spirit of dread, which was hindering me from all that God had purposed for my life. In the beginning of my ministry, I held nightly services in my home and people would come declaring they needed assistance with personal obligations. Because I was and am very compassionate, I felt obligated to help them. I did not want to see anyone get evicted, go without food, or have their electricity disconnected, so I would help. I probably helped "more than I should have" because some people took that kindness for weakness. They took advantage of my desire to help.

It wasn't until one evening service, God sent my future husband, Bishop M.B. Jefferson, to speak a word into my life. He told me about the people, the fears, and those things which had me bound. Then he told me about the calling on my life and where God was about to take me. When the Bishop prayed over me, I could feel the anointing and the shackles loosen. Everything that had me bound immediately released from me and was replaced by feelings of joy, peace, and liberty. From that day onwards, my life has never been the same.

It is interesting because as a child my faith was incredibly strong. Yet, as grew older, my foundation seemed to be rocked by life itself. Yet, that wonderful night at the service when Bishop showed up, it was a miracle; and that miraculous experience caused me to function at a higher level of faith than ever before. I believed God at His Word! He gave me a plan and in obedience to His Word; I made a commitment to follow His plan. I listen when God speaks, and I acknowledge Him. Fear or no fear, I remained steadfast and unmovable in obtaining my goals through Christ.

There are several instances where I had to remove doubt and develop the faith to float. I'm almost positive in some instances when I stepped out on what God inspired me to do, that some thought I had lost my natural mind. I recall the time when I was selling thousands of donuts a day. It seemed impossible to others, but I believed God and the plan He had given me to bring finances into the ministry. There was another time when I called on God, I heard the voice of the Lord, "Place three peanuts in a bag, ask the priest to bless them, and then go out." I knew it was the voice of God speaking. He told me to tell the people, the peanuts were blessed and when they bless God's House, their prayers will be answered. To some it seemed strange, but to me I remembered what God said, "For my thoughts are not your thoughts, neither are your ways my ways, saith the Lord. For as the Heavens are higher than the Earth, so are my ways higher than your ways, and my thoughts than your thoughts," (Isa. 55:8-9).

When a team of us went out in faith, people were blessing us with 50-100 dollars at a time, for the three blessed peanuts. Not just any peanuts, but *blessed* peanuts. God gave the people hope. God did it, we just obeyed! It was not about the quantity of the peanuts in the bag; it was the quality. It was about the blessing in the bag. We told the people in faith to receive their healing when they eat the blessed peanuts. We told everyone that donated that blessings of healing, deliverance, and salvation would come to them and their loved ones. They believed God and blessed His House. When I reflect back to the time of the three peanuts, I sincerely thank God for His wondrous works. Some people came back looking for us after they ate the peanuts, and shared their testimony of how God blessed them after receiving the bag. Some even gave more money and requested more "blessed" peanuts.

No matter how strange, faith requires you to believe even when something seems unbelievable. Stand on His Word! When God speaks to your heart, no matter how strange it might appear to be to man, doubt not! There are numerous situations in the Bible where God instructed one of His servants to do a task or gave them an assignment, and what was requested seemed strange. Look at Hezekiah. He had boils all over his body. God's servant, Isaiah, told Hezekiah to take a lump of fig leaves and lay them over the boils and he would be healed. I can imagine some people thought that was a *strange* thing to do. Yet, Hezekiah's body recovered from the boils because he believed and did not doubt (2 Kgs. 20).

In another instance, Elijah traveled to Zarephath. When he arrived at the city gate, a widow woman was gathering sticks. He called out to her and asked her for some water. As she was fetching the water, he then asked her to bring him a little piece of bread in her hand. She told God's servant Elijah that she had no cake, only a handful of flour, a little oil, and that is why she was gathering the sticks. She was planning to cook the bread for her and her son. Elijah told the woman not to be afraid and to go ahead and make him some bread, and after that make some for her and her son. The woman did as Elijah said, and the three ate for many days (1 Kgs. 17:10-15).

The woman did not doubt, and she did exactly what Elijah requested. As a result, her household was blessed.

God has always moved in peculiar ways in my life. Once, I dreamed about a building with the inscription "The House of...." In my dream, I could not see the remaining words. The next morning, when I mentioned my dream to Bishop Jefferson, he said that the last word was David—The House of David. It turned out that both Bishop and I had the same dream. We were both given the charge to open a residential facility for men, women, and families whose lives have been altered by drugs, alcohol, prostitution, domestic violence, hopelessness, and other such issues. That facility was to be named "The House of

David." These houses are a city of refuge for the outcast to find salvation, healing, and deliverance.

As we taught the Word of God and provided for the people, God met all of our needs. He blessed us with multiple properties, some of which we purchased, and others were donated. The properties served as residences, for the people God sent to us for help. Some properties had to be renovated to accommodate the people; but God provided everything we needed to accomplish that goal. There are no fees or charges to be a resident within the House of David. We believed God and surely, the dream came to pass. At one time, the population grew to over 400 residents. It is not funded by government grants or loans; instead, it was maintained by God. We received everything we needed through free-will offerings and partnerships. Our assignment was to teach the people the Word of God. We preached and taught the unadulterated TRUTH!

Although God ordained the House of David, it doesn't mean it came about or existed without trials. Along the way, preconceived thoughts crept up in some people's minds. This happened on both a local and national level. It's unfortunate that many tend to believe the worst about others, especially within a body of believers. However, all someone has to do is examine carefully what is being said, to ascertain the truth. Regardless of the murmurings, we overcame the naysayers and remained focused on what God called us to do. We walked in agreement with God and regardless of what the media said, regardless of what others said, we continued to move forward in obedience.

Had it not been for our faith, we would have given up a long time ago and this ministry would not be. When I reflect on Psalm 66:8-20, I have to give God thanks because He allowed so much to go unnoticed by us. We went through a lot. Many turned their backs on us. There were times we were so discouraged, not understanding why we were having such difficulty in helping other people. I questioned God often. Yet by persevering and continuing on, I gained insight on my struggle.

In the Bible, God says, "Fear thou not; for I am with thee: be not dismayed; for I am thy God: I will strengthen thee; yea, I will help thee…" (Isa. 41:10). He allowed us to go through the fire (trial), yet we overcame our difficulty (test) and came out of it unscathed. Although many attempted to charge us with much wrong-doing, God still prevailed. We continued to give thanks during the struggle and we never bowed down to another god. God had a plan, and His plan is always greater than the enemy's scheme.

WORDS OF EMPOWERMENT

1. Be strong in the Lord, and in the power of His might. Put on the whole armor of God, so you can withstand the tactics of the devil. Take the breastplate of righteousness, the belt of Truth, the shield of faith, the helmet of salvation, the sword of the spirit, and prepare your feet with the gospel of peace.

2. Stop looking and questioning which direction God shall come from. He will shower you with His blessings. Remain open to receive them and be thankful because He will never cease to amaze you. SMILE!

3. Don't allow failures to keep you down. As the saying goes, "Nothing beats a failure but a try!" When you fall down, get back up and try, try, try again.

4. Remain focus on your goals and never ever take your eye off your vision.

5. Have faith because God has placed within each of us creative "mojo." Activate your faith through your works.

6. God deposits specific goals into His children as they pursue their purpose throughout life. When you walk in God's wisdom, He charts a plan for you to accomplish those goals.

7. If you don't have a specific goal, ask God to give you one. Everyone has purpose in the body of Christ.

8. If things are not going as you desire them to go and you are not manifesting in your life and you would hope to, do an analysis. Do a self-examination to see if your timing aligns with God's timing.

9. It is always a good idea to consult with those you trust and who support your vision. Your spiritual mentors or guides, as well as the pastors of your church, might lend a listening ear and provide you with sound counsel. Don't be afraid to seek them out for guidance and/or advice.

10. Don't allow the enemy to frustrate your purpose. Study Ezra 4 as an example of what can happen if you are not on watch and prayerful.

11. Keep your heart in the right place. Walk in the Truth, in the light, and never compromise your integrity. By living truthfully, God will subdue your enemies and protect you.

12. Be careful who you share information with because everyone does not support and/or understand what you have been called to do.

COURSE EIGHT DAILY AFFIRMATIONS

- There are no limits in God; therefore, I shall remain faithful!
- God is using me, and He can do miraculous and mighty things in and through me.
- I will allow God to hold me up by His righteous hand.
- I have no doubt in my abilities because my God stands with me.
- In everything, I seek God's wisdom.
- I serve a BIG God with BIG ideas.
- I will continue to press toward the mark for the prize of the high calling of God in Jesus Christ.

- God continuously blesses me through my obedience to Him.
- Even against all odds, I shall not deter from my assignment and calling from God.
- God gave me His Word and it shall not return void in my life.
- I do not doubt God.
- I have the faith to float.

Study Scriptures to Strengthen You

1 Chronicles 28:20

Hebrews 11:6

1 Chronicles 28:19

Malachi 2:7

Ecclesiastes 3:11

Ezra 4:5

Acts 17:28

2 Kings 20

1 Kings 17

Proverbs 3:5-6

Psalm 66:8-20

1 Samuel 2:35

Isaiah 55:10-11

Course 9

The Dream Must Be Organized in a Programmatic Format

"And Joshua said unto the children of Israel, How long are ye slack to go to possess the land, which the Lord God of your fathers hath given you?" (Josh.18:3).

"But thou shalt remember the Lord thy God: for it is He that giveth thee power to get wealth, that He may establish His covenant which He sware unto thy fathers, as it is this day," (Deut. 8:18).

At last, we are towards the end of this journey. This is the final course, and I would like to discuss the importance of organizing your ideas, goals, and objectives, so you can better bring your dreams to fruition. Therefore, in Course Nine, the guiding principle is: *The dream must be organized in a programmatic format.*

Countless people have turned their dreams into reality, and lived or are living a successful life. Success is like beauty— it is in the eye of the beholder. Regardless of the success achieved, it is noted that many were born into it, while others have had to work hard to achieve it. Each of those individuals surely have a dynamic testimony to share.

In history, Abraham Lincoln dreamed of being the President of the United States. Despite many setbacks and trials, he lived to become president. In 1862, he is credited to having said, "Whatever shall appear to be God's will, I will do."

In retrospect, God has brought me through adversity, and I can see how blessed I am. Although the journey has not always been a smooth one, and although the prelude to my victories, were the trials, the truth is I claimed the victory with God's help. Yes, I was presented with obstacles, yet I knew God would bring me out. From a historical context, President Lincoln was controversial to some, and to others a major motivation behind the movement to free slaves. Regardless of other political factors that exist, his words are relevant. "Amid the greatest difficulties of my administration, when I could not see any other resort, I would place my whole reliance in God, knowing that all would go well and that He would decide for the right." It doesn't matter if I or others respect the former president, his words ring true.

There are many famous and not so many famous people, who out of necessity set goals to bring about changes in the way things worked. In their endeavors, many invented ways to do things just a little bit more efficiently. For instance, Garret Morgan, is most famous for his inventions of the gas mask and the traffic signal. Lewis Latimer, an inventor and draftsman, whose parents fled slavery when he was young, significantly contributed to patenting the lightbulb and the telephone. He not only assisted others with their projects, but he also invented a few of his own, two significant ones being "an improved railroad car bathroom and an early air conditioning unit." Famous brothers, Orville and Wilbur Wright's contributions help us today in the "friendly skies" as they have been credited with inventing one of the original airplanes. George Washington Carver took a tiny nut to a whole new level by creating various by-products from the peanut. And the dreamer himself, the Reverend Dr. Martin Luther King, Jr. had a dream that one day his children would live in a nation where they would not be judged by the color of their skin, but by the content of their character. Unfortunately, Dr. King's dream ended too soon, but his legacy lives on. In lieu of his efforts, children across the nation reap the benefit of integrated play and learning.

When you dare to dream big, don't forget to prepare for adversity. You will be talked about, misunderstood, and criticized. Use that to propel you to a greater dependence on God. When afflicted and it seems as if everything is coming against you, rest assured that the suffering is strengthening you. In 1 Peter 5:10 it states, "But the God of all grace, who hath called us unto His eternal glory by Christ Jesus, after that ye have suffered a while, make you perfect, stablish, strengthen, settle you."

The famous people mentioned above, and ones not named, all of their successes were achieved because they had a plan. Better yet, God had a plan. It was not achieved haphazardly. Each person became successful because they took action, persevered despite setbacks, and followed the guidance of God.

Looking back, Noah built the Ark during a dry season. He was mocked, laughed at, and called crazy. Yet, he stayed the course until the Ark was complete. He rallied those who believed with him and put them to work. The objective — Complete the Building of the Ark! The workers did not just pull together some lumber, nails, hammer, and tools. No! They developed a plan from the vision that Moses received from God.

This situation is no different with you. To achieve what God has placed in your heart to do, you must put a plan together and then ultimately, execute that plan. God has blessed me tremendously in ministry, in business, and in my personal life. I not only trusted God, but I kept the faith no matter what came my way. I did not trust in my own ability to bring about success, I trusted in God's ability to make things happen in my life. I had to be about the work and take action to bring it into fruition. Every person I have ever been blessed to know, who has achieved anything great in their life, they will tell you they have been "tested and tried." However, no matter what came their way, they fought for their success; they pushed through every hardship and continued pushing until they succeeded.

It helps to have encouraging words along the way. It helps to be in the midst of people who believe in you and believe in your vision. God encircled me with many people who served as confirmation of His will. My stylist, Ray Parker, was in a swimming pool when he said God told him to call and tell me "it costs nothing to dream." Then my children, Pastor Calvin and Ninkia came each at different times giving me messages about fulfilling my dreams and achieving whatever you set your mind to do. When I received each word, I knew without a doubt that God was speaking through them.

I have had many ideas of things to accomplish. I have had many visions of things that God has instructed me to do. One thing that God placed on my heart, was to help women change their mindset about their health. God said, "If you make them healthy, I will make them wealthy." In observing the dietary habits of the women around me, particularly those who were in ministry and close to me, I noticed how they would inhale a lot of junk food. It bothered me, as I witnessed their lack of energy because of various health challenges, such as hypertension and diabetes. I cried out to God on what to do. I wanted for them to reach their full potential and develop a healthier lifestyle. I thought to myself, "there is no way I can help them feel good about themselves." I know from experience that when you feel good about yourself, you are more productive. I wanted to inspire these women to value themselves, to show them the importance of self-care and how to treat themselves better.

When I sought God's wisdom and guidance, I had a dream about a building furnished with state-of-the-art equipment. It had a sauna, spa, skin care salon, and massage chairs. The atmosphere of this building was very peaceful and inviting. It was luxurious and upscale. God showed me what I needed to do to make this dream a reality and help the women, but He also reminded me that victory is a mindset. He said, "You have to set your mind to be a winner. You have to move on up your mountain. You can do it."

What I understood in all of this was, that when women are healthy they can successfully fulfill their roles in ministry, at home, and in business. The dream became a reality and the **Who Cares? We Care Center** was born out of a yearning in my heart to help women in ministry. I had to do some work though! It didn't just pop up out of nowhere. It seemed the more I worked toward the manifestation of the goal, the more opposition that came up against me. The enemy did not want to see the ladies healthy. He desired to keep the mission of Christ entangled and delayed. His job is to kill, to steal, and to destroy. Yet, my eyes were fixed on Heaven and I set my mind on things above because I knew what God had promised. I refused to look at trouble and instead I looked at God, for I knew without a doubt He was and is able to finish that which He had begun. I was determined for the dream to come to pass. So, once I fixed my mindset, the resources poured in. This was not about me! It was about God's people and His desire to help them change their condition. God put legs on that dream and inspired me with a plan in which some thought was ludicrous.

The Who Cares? We Care Center was placed dead smack in the middle of a community infested with crime, drugs, and violence. It's there even today and it's a place where people can exercise, learn to eat healthy, relax, forget about all the cares of the world, and receive pampering. But like I said, this building didn't just appear out of nowhere. We labored to bring it about! There were days and nights, I would go over to the center and walk around praying to my Father. I gave Him back His Word and knew He was faithful to perform it! I didn't sit still but I put on my work clothes, got a bucket of putty, some tile for the walls and worked. Being inexperienced in laying tile did not stop me. It was God doing it through me; I was just the vessel. Some of the ladies stopped by the center and saw me fully committed to the task. "Dr. Brenda, you're putting your hands down in that putty?" Yes, I was!

I could not sit back without putting works to my faith. I could have looked at the walls all day, waiting for them to be covered with tile but I knew there would not be a finished product without works. I couldn't continue to wait on others to help me do the job. God gave it. Others didn't necessarily see my dream the way God gave it to me; therefore the same urgency didn't exist. Like I said, I was determined to complete it, just like Noah was determined to finish building the Ark. The Who Cares? We Care facility is a blessing to the community. We are dedicated to working with those who will set their minds for victory and seek to refresh themselves, holistically. We are committed to the process of a healthy transformation for every individual: mind, body, and spirit. When you enter our doors, we welcome you and will run with you towards your health goal, all the way to the finish line. We care about your overall well-being.

Another idea I've had since youth was to own my own clothing line. I have always enjoyed working with fashion and style. Sewing suits by hand for men and women yesterday, has since turned into owning a boutique today, called 'Brenda by Design.' With this dream, I kept the faith. This one did not come about by just wishing it into existence. Again, it took work, a plan, and working that plan!

Many people do not understand why our ministry focuses on learning and knowing God's Word. As leaders of a blessed congregation, for my husband and I, our jobs are different but parallel to each other. Bishop Jefferson ministers the spoken Word of God and I minister the Word of God through songs. I do not sing. When I began writing scripture songs, I knew nothing about music, not a note or a pitch. Yet, I believed in my dream. I prayed to God for an understanding of pure and true praise and worship.

"But none saith, where is God my maker, who giveth songs in the night?" (Job 35:10).

I knew the Word of God. I did not question Him asking, "Are you sure? Are you talking about me?" When God speaks, even the wind and the raging sea has to obey. I knew the voice of the Lord. It was God all by Himself. In my endeavors to pursue music, there were many critics and those who thought it to be a joke.

Nevertheless, I still followed God. In my obedience, God sat me in position before great gospel talent and artists. People I would have never imagined having their acquaintance and favor, these individuals helped me to fulfill my commandment from God. When the favor of God is upon your life, doors swing open for your dreams to be manifested. My boast is in God, for He did it all by Himself. He receives the glory for the artists, producers, psalmists, musicians, and singers who have helped me to embrace my dreams, by His permission.

"Who is this Dr. Brenda Jefferson and where did she come from?" I smile when I hear whispers because I know it was not me, but the God in me who allowed me to do great things in His name. I give God all the glory and all the praise. In the midnight hours, when riding in a car or on a plane, I sometimes can hear the Word come forth in sweet melodies in my heart. Like the pen of a ready writer, I write the songs as God reveals them. Through the Holy Spirit, I'm inspired to compose and have produced hundreds of powerful scripture songs. God even blessed me with a music label, "Scripture Music Group." The anointed lyrics from God have allowed me to be connected with the best in the gospel industry. God said in His Word, your gifts will make room for you and bring you before great men (Prov. 18:16). I believe in the power of God. He can and will bring your dream to pass. Again, it did not just come about by coincidence or chance. It took work and a plan, and the ability to work that plan to fulfill His will.

God gave me a dream to begin a new group, Pure & True Praise. I sought faithful members in our congregation who desired to learn God's Word and praise Him from a pure heart. These singers did not have to possess former training or vocal abilities, but sincere hearts to sing His Word. God told me to teach them His Word through the songs and teach them to live Holy. He said if their hearts are pure as they praise; He would cover their vocals. God said He would cover their faults with His anointing and a trained ear would never recognize their deficiencies. God did just as He said. We turned no one down who wanted to be a part of Pure & True Praise. If they desired Holiness, God said; help them learn His Word. God gave them an affirmation: "O Lord my God. I submit to your will. I vow to live a life of Holiness. I pledge to forever give you praise from a pure heart. Lifting and clapping my hands, I will sing your Word with power. I make a covenant with you, O Lord to be a vessel of praise; releasing the anointing to set the captives free. I will exhort your name in spirit and in truth."

As this affirmation became a part of their daily testimony, we saw the lives of the singers transform. Our small group soon became a choir. If I would have listened to those who doubted my vision, my dreams would have died. Each song God has given me is a testimony of His goodness. The lyrics and inspirational messages were birthed from life experiences.

There have been many ideas and businesses along the way, each having their own season. From laundry facilities to restaurants, tire shops, ice cream parlors, we have done it all. For every dream I pursued, there was a battle prior to it coming to pass. Yet, I did not allow trouble, fear, or doubt to hinder me. When the pieces didn't fit together, I did not become frustrated, instead I kept working until my vision was realized and manifested tangibly.

During a season of my walk with God, I became ill and was taken to the hospital. The doctors discovered that I had blood-clots on my heart, lungs, and liver. They were negative in their prognosis, and gave little hope of my total recovery; but little did they know that my hope was in God, and not in their prognosis. God spoke a Word through Bishop Jefferson; "[You] shall not die, but live, and declare the works of the Lord," (Ps. 118:17). God then sent a young physician and he provided treatment and a positive word. He told me "Go live your life and see the beauty of the world."

From that experience, the *Time of Refreshing* album was birthed. God said, "Put pain and troubles behind me, it's a new day and a new year. It's Time!" God told me to get up from the hospital bed, fix myself up, and be about His business. His business is bringing souls into His House, bringing in the downtrodden and outcast, providing them with shelter and hope.

So, as we discussed, this Course is about organizing your dream and putting it into a programmatic format. You might be asking, "What is that exactly?" A programmatic format is a plan in which to monetize your vision. A plan to make your dream a reality. There is a list of things to do in creating your plan.

MAKING YOUR DREAM A REALITY

1. **Position yourself for your dream to come to pass.** Positioning yourself is about establishing a specific mindset to claim the victory. God invests in those He can trust to diligently stay the course and complete the task. Position yourself around those who embrace your

dream, and those fulfilling their own dreams. Position yourself with those who trust God and obey Him. When you visualize your dreams, activate them with faith and works. What the mind can conceive and believe can be achieved. If you cannot visualize your dreams, how will others? Without a vision the people perish. Act upon your dreams with clear vision. Understand it and work the unseen until it materializes. You may receive your dream in measures but in time; it will come together. Just like a puzzle, if the pieces do not immediately fit; eventually, they will. Your job is to keep the pursuit. In the end, the full picture seen on the box will come into view. For a dream cometh through the multitude of business; and a fool's voice is known by multitude of words (Eccl. 5:3). Continue to move into your purpose and stand on the Word of God.

2. **Create a list of what you want to accomplish.** Write everything out and keep it before you. Place them on your wall, refrigerator, in your car, bathroom or wherever you can be reminded of them daily.

3. **Write your vision.** Write out your vision fully as you can visualize it. Create a vision board to see it more clearly (Hab. 2:2).

4. **Seek Godly counsel.** Seek God on the beginning of each project (Mal. 2:7). "Blessed is the man that walketh not in the counsel of the ungodly…" (Ps. 1:1).

5. **Establish a support team/accountability partners.** Surround yourself with people of faith and who believe in your dreams.

6. **Stay prayerful and listen to God's guidance.** God inspires through various avenues. Listen, watch, and pray. Stop and pray for at least 60 seconds at the top of each hour, giving reverence to God for the other 59 minutes.

7. **Create an action plan to accomplish your goals.** Create action steps and complete daily progress toward your goals and stay the course!

When you write things down, you are in essence creating a roadmap to follow. It helps you to put action behind your vision to manifest them. Your destiny is awaiting you. Your faith and obedience will ignite a spark within, to create a forward motion.

WORDS OF EMPOWERMENT

1. Continue to dream and have faith in God. When the winds are blowing, abide in the ship. God is a comforter, and He will never give you more than you can bear (2 Cor. 1:3-10).

2. Live in the perfect will of God. Seek His guidance through His Word, fasting, and prayer. When you walk in the will of God, He will never make you to look ashamed.

3. The faith in God will cause you to stretch beyond the ordinary limits and reach into the unthinkable.
4. It is vital to move when God speaks. Do not draw back.

5. God is the Creator of all things, be grateful and thankful that He has chosen you as a vessel to carry out His work on Earth. Keep your heart aligned to His.

6. God wants to bless you. Remain faithful. Do not accept failure. Allow your plan to unfold exactly how it is supposed to. Remember things happen on God's time, and He has perfect timing. Seek God's wisdom and wait on Him.

7. Victory is a mindset. Therefore, you have to set your mind to do what you have dreamed of doing.

8. When the sufferings of Christ abound, God steps in as a comforter. He is our consolation. We have to remain steadfast knowing that when we are afflicted, we are partakers of the same suffering as Christ.

9. In the innermost part of your being, there is a yearning for greater. Whatever God has given you; He will guide you into achieving it.
10. Be encouraged today to set your mind to be a winner.

11. If you have stopped dreaming, be encouraged today to dream again. No matter what is going on, what has happened in your past, or what the future appears to hold for you; live out your dream! God is bigger than any hindrance seeking to stop you.

12. Your dreams are like a baby being born; you have to push hard to birth and get your blessing through despite the pain.

COURSE NINE DAILY AFFIRMATIONS

- God makes the impossible possible.
- Faith, virtue, knowledge, temperance, patience, Godliness, brotherly kindness, and charity are characteristics I must have as I walk on my path. I will think and act on these things.
- I dream, take action, and achieve because I think outside of the box.
- I shall not procrastinate or be defeated!
- God's ability shines forth through me and I have total dependence on Him.
- God is the great I AM, my El Shaddai, my all and all.
- I owe all my victory to God. The glory belongs to Him.
- There is a perfect season for everything God assigns for me, and I am walking in that season right now.
- I will not turn away from my dreams.

- God is my comforter, and He does not give me more than I can handle.

- I am enthusiastic about my dreams and the ability to achieve them.

- I believe in myself and therefore I step out on faith.

- God will direct my steps when I move forward to possess the land.

Study Scriptures to Strengthen You

Joel 2:27

Psalm 121:1-2

Genesis 37:5-11

1 Chronicles 28

Hebrews 11:1

Ecclesiastes 11:1

Hebrews 11:30

Joshua 6:3-13

1 Peter 5:10

2 Corinthians 1:3-10

Conclusion

Throughout this journey, we have discussed principles to consider regarding achieving success in your life as you pursue your dreams. In *Course 1* we shared that "*God and His Word is An Anchor*." We have to move over and let God take the stern or driver's seat, allowing Him to have control over our lives. In *Course 2, "Praise Him While I Wait,"* we discussed the power and purpose of your praise. How to use it as a weapon against the enemy and as a seed for increase. *Course 3* encouraged us to "*Remove Ungodly Strongholds*." The enemy uses the same tactics to kill, steal, and destroy, yet we are made free in Christ. The presiding point of this principle is to remove any doubt, negativity, and strongholds through the power of prayer, praise, and meditation. In *Course 4* we introduced the principle, "*The Seed of Righteousness*." The overall message was to allow the spirit of love to be at the root of everything you do. In *Course 5* we stressed the importance of understanding that you must "*Unchain Your Mind*." In this course the discussion, we centered on the need to remove limiting belief systems and faulty thinking.

The principle of *Course 6* is "*Clarify Your Dreams*." The commentary in this Course guided you to not only go beyond the surface of your ideas, but also to be honest and clear about what it is you desire. *Course 7* introduced the principle, "*Align Your Dreams with God's Purpose.*" In this particular Course, you were encouraged to discover the connection between your earnest dreams and yearnings, to the purpose that God has for your life. This course caused you to examine yourself and your connection to Almighty God. *Course 8*'s principle is, "*Remove Doubt and Develop the Faith to Float*, which presented information about how faith is indeed an activator in achieving what you desire in your life. Finally, *Course 9* principle is, "*The Dream Must Be Organized in a Programmatic Format.*" The premise behind this principle is organizing your ideas and your visions into an action plan so you are not simply dreaming about achieving something in your life. It gives insight on how to put motion behind your ideas, taking daily measures of action to ultimately accomplish them step-by-step.

At the onset of this journey, you were urged to not only be encouraged, but also to understand that with every challenge, obstacle, or problem that arises, that there is also a solution or an answer. You were admonished to have a strong conviction about what you stand for and have the faith to know that what you desire of God is already done.

The poignant point of this entire book is to dream big, keep the faith, and place God and His Word at the forefront of all that you do.

God's plan for our lives is far greater than any plan we can develop on our own accord. As we come into the knowledge and understanding of His Word, we gain strength and foresight. When the Word of God dwells in our heart, it brings forth an abundant life in Christ. It is, however, pertinent that you understand that obedience usually comes prior to understanding. Contrary to some folk's belief systems, God desires us to be happy and prosperous, not to live in lack, sickness, discouragement, depression, or oppression.

There should never be a moment in the life of any believer in which the circumstances of the carnal world distract your focus from God. No matter the situation or circumstance, you have control over everything happening in your life. You created your circumstances with your thoughts, words, and actions! From the moment you speak a word, you give birth to results. As the saying goes, "there is nothing new under the sun," therefore, do not allow the schemes and machinations of the enemy to displace you from the foot of Jesus. One touch from the Master's hand can change your circumstances in phenomenal ways. Study the passage 1 Peter 1:5-10. Also, remember the lesson of Ecclesiastes 9:11 as you press forward to the achievement of your dreams and goals. Remember that the race is not to the swift or the strong, but to those who can endure until the end.

Through the trials and struggles we face along life's journey; we gain wisdom, and it is our testimony of deliverance that we can then share with others. In this way, we become a living epistle of God's glory and become more grounded in Him. So, I can tell you that you must keep going in the face of opposition until you see your dream come to fruition. Remain steadfast and keep the faith because in the sanctuary of God, there is a river of blessings which overflows and provides unimaginable opportunities. Just continue to speak life into your home, your situation, and your dreams. God supernaturally blesses your storehouse; therefore, you must look past your current condition and see the end result of your dream. As a child of God, you are a producer, and as long as you keep believing and keep progressing in the way of your idea, it will undoubtedly come to fruition. You will, with God's help, ultimately develop techniques and generate ideas that will bring you tangible results and profit. Work your plan and be prepared to receive the blessings of the Lord in your life.

Some Scriptures to remember are Ezekiel 47:3-10; Numbers 23:19; Hebrews 4:9; Philippians 2:5; and Romans 2:11.

Know the great God you serve, take a stand, and take your place in God. Go get your inheritance!

You may ask, "Who this great God I serve?" I shall tell you!

- Adonai-Jehovah -- The Lord our Sovereign
- El-Elyon -- The Lord Most High
- El-Olam -- The Everlasting God
- El-Shaddai -- The God who is sufficient for the needs of His people
- Jehovah-Elohim -- The Eternal Creator
- Jehovah-Jireh -- The Lord our Provider
- Jehovah-Nissi -- The Lord our Banner
- Jehovah-Rapha -- The Lord our Healer
- Jehovah-Shalom -- The Lord our Peace
- Jehovah-Tsidkenu -- The Lord our Righteousness
- Jehovah-Mekaddishkem -- The Lord our Sanctifier
- Jehovah-Sabaoth -- The Lord of Hosts
- Jehovah-Shammah -- The Lord is Present
- Jehovah-Rohi -- The Lord our Shepherd
- Jehovah-Eloheenu -- The Lord our God

God is everything you need Him to be in your life. So dream, dream on! Speak your dreams out of your mouth. It's in you, so dream, it shall come to pass. If you believe your dream, you can achieve your dream. As you follow the principles in this book and you start seeing the flow happening in your life, remember what I told you! The vision shall come to pass. Every morning I rise, I look with anticipation of seeing my dreams unfold. I reflect on what God has done in my life:

- New edifice for worship - Deeper Life Christian Church
- Second edifice for worship – Living in Victory Christian Church
- Deeper Life Christian School
- Youth Enrichment Center
- New House of David Help Center
- Daycare Centers
- Restaurant

So as you turn the page and close this book, it is not the end, but truly a magnificent beginning to a whole new chapter in your life. God's Speed!

"And David said to Solomon his son, Be strong and of good courage, and do it: fear not, nor be dismayed: for the Lord God, even my God, will be with thee; He will not fail thee, nor forsake thee, until thou hast finished all the work for the service of the house of the Lord," (1 Chr. 28:20).

My Prayer

Father, I thank you for every reader. I ask that you bring forth a miraculous shift in the spiritual realm which will manifest that which you have spoken in their lives. Allow your Word to penetrate their hearts to bring inspiration and vitality, so that they may persevere in the midst of adversity. Like the dew in the morning, gently rest upon their hearts. For we know in your rest is everything we need.

Father, I thank you for my husband, Bishop M.B. Jefferson and for the anointing you have placed upon his life to lead your people in Truth. Thank you for each dream you have allowed us to see manifest and unfold. I give you all the glory for doing it, for you are God and you dwell in the midst of your people.

In Jesus' name, I pray. *Amen.*

About the Author

Born in Tampa, Florida, Dr. Brenda Jefferson is an overcomer. Facing many trials, tribulations, and the spirit of fear,

it was through God's Word that Dr. Jefferson was transformed and evolved into a living epistle; a walking demonstration of Holy boldness.

Dr. Jefferson, who holds a PhD in Biblical Theology, met Bishop M.B. Jefferson at the age of 25 and the two began working in ministry together. Dr. Jefferson who was living in Quincy, Florida at the time the Bishop established a church in Quincy, soon began pastoring in that church. Eventually, Bishop Jefferson and Dr. Jefferson became married.

To date, the dynamic duo have been serving in ministry for 45 years catering to those who have been broken, struggling with addictions, abuse, those lost and in despair. Committed to taking the gospel to the nations, Dr. Brenda Jefferson believes in taking ministry to the next level. An award-winning songwriter and producer, she is the CEO of Scripture Music Group. Dr. Brenda has worked with some of the gospel industry's best such as Lisa Page Brooks, Lecresia Campbell, Damita Haddon, Beverly Crawford, Gerald and Tammi Haddon, Rance Allen, Dorinda

Clark-Cole, Donald Lawrence, Kurt Carr, and Vickie Winans to name a few. Her latest releases: *Triumph through Pain, Invocation* and *Supernatural* are now available on all digital outlets and can be heard in ministries nationwide.

Other Works by Dr. Brenda Jefferson

Books:

Rhema Through My Song

Triumph through Pain

A Time of Refreshing

Dreams Come True

Hast Thou Not Known

The Blue Diamond in You

The Pen of a Ready Writer

Songs from the Heart

Music Albums:

Triumph through Pain

Invocation

A Time of Refreshing

Album Single(s) Released:

Supernatural

Oh Clap your Hands

Visit Dr. Brenda Jefferson Online:

www.BrendaJefferson.com

Also, you can purchase Music Albums, additional Singles, and the "Rhema through My Song" Book through various other digital online platforms.